T0157131

I Never Knew My Place

Living, Surviving, and Thinking in a Subservient Society

Eleanor Curry

iUniverse, Inc.
Bloomington

I Never Knew My Place
Living, Surviving, and Thinking
in a Subservient Society

iUniverse books may be ordered through booksellers or by contacting:

iUniverse
1663 Liberty Drive
Bloomington, IN 47403
www.iuniverse.com
1-800-Authors (1-800-288-4677)

ISBN: 978-1-4759-1627-0 (sc)
ISBN: 978-1-4759-1628-7 (e)

Printed in the United States of America

iUniverse rev. date: 7/3/2012

ALSO BY ELEANOR CURRY
Letters to My Granddaughter
Courageous Person's Guide to Friendship
A Liberated Woman from the Ghetto
Racial Stories

Contents

Foreword

You are about to embark upon an adventure into the mind and spirit of Eleanor Williams-Curry. You will see how she creates for her kids and us a guide to dealing with the struggles of life through the use of charm, joy, wisdom, and wit.

Our friendship began one night in 1966, at the close of a meeting with community leaders. The topic was exploring the desegregation of the San Mateo Elementary School District. I asked her if she needed a ride home. After three hours of consuming lots of tea, and a multitude of days beyond that, our bond was forever sealed. As the saying goes, "We cannot pick our relatives, but we can pick our friends." I believe God picked my friend Eleanor for me because he knew I needed her to be a part of my life. Over the span of forty-six years, I have found Eleanor to be one of the wisest, most insightful, and most loving people God has put on this earth. She manages to maneuver through the maze of life's twists and turns, and her children certainly recognize her morals and values. Through this memoir, you will see how she feels and thinks too.

Eleanor gives us a treasure chest filled with compelling testimony on the power of God's love exhibited through her. This translates into harmony regardless of perplexing times, raising her family, and working in her civic, community services. She never doubts God's existence or strays from his teachings. She spreads his powerful messages with excitement and exuberance. She has conquered fear and doesn't ever appear to fail herself or others.

"The best thing that has ever happened to me is being born at this time in history and being born a person of color in the U.S.A." Eleanor stated this in 1974.

She believes "it is extremely necessary to develop a flexible attitude, a receptive mind, to be tough, to be gentle, and to get along with each other."

This latest effort puts together a philosophical picture of a woman with an indomitable spirit, a powerful will, and an extraordinary grasp of common sense. You will be inspired, you will laugh, you will cry, and most of all, you will find Eleanor unforgettable.

Jill Wakeman

Acknowledgments

My family is the center of my life. Richmond Earl Curry, my husband, waited, watched, and wondered as I spent countless hours preparing my life's story. Now that our children are adults, each has a precise internal spirit of caring for me, different from one another. Their names are Brenda, Bonnie (deceased), Barbara, Richmond, Jr., Arnold, William, Paul, and David. I marvel at their insight as they do various things that cause me to receive heartfelt love, which enhances my life. Thanks to my beloved close-knit family.

I also want to thank Jill Wakeman for her time and inquiring mind. Her openness caused me to go deeper before one word was written. A book titled *The Help* made me realize it was time for my story. After seeing the movie, I know that now is the time to share; we as "people of color" are visible and viable, and we volunteer to build our communities. Double thanks to you, Jill.

Claire Mack, former and first African American mayor of the City of San Mateo is a woman whom I appreciate and respect for introducing me to other mentors and broadening my base of influence with agents, workshops program classes, and other professional writers.

Just as important with their valuable support are Carl Brown, Ethel Burnside, Barbara Conway, Carmeleit

Delaney-Oakes, Rev. Larry Wayne Ellis, Joanne Griffin, Lenneal Henderson's family, Monica Hollands, Erma Prothro, Thomas Ruppanner, Rhonda Robinson, Anita Webb, Rev. Clifford Williams, and my mother, Ophelia Thornton-Williams.

Jeanne Jangier, former creative writing instructor at the College of San Mateo, became my master reader and proofreader. Jeanne is amazing with her extensive knowledge.

I hope you find another portion of American history as perceived by people living it day by day in our own words.

Introduction

I Never Knew My Place takes me deep into experiences about my own life that I have seldom taken time to ponder, until now.

Do you realize that the shadows of our lives that appear hidden always show up in the light? Without light, there would be no shadows. We are so busy "doing" that we forget to "be." The complexities and competitiveness of the broad world cause us to avoid or ignore our individual worlds. However, we cannot let the world squeeze us into its mold.

I am very comfortable in my own culture, yet I continue to seek out people who are different. I appreciate and understand others as I discover more of myself. More similarities exist among us than we care to admit. The key to good living, according to Shakespeare, is to "know thyself." We have to closely examine and live our own lives. It is not about the material things we accumulate, the toys we have, the money we hoard, or the illnesses we might endure. Instead, think, "Did somebody help me when I needed it? Did I help anybody when they needed it?"

The *International Who's Who of Professionals* (1998) has the following data:

Eleanor Williams-Curry
President
African American Community Entrustment
50 California Street, #200
San Francisco, Ca. 94111

Business Information: Based in San Francisco, African American Community Entrustment raises and distributes funds for the African American community. The agency's effects revolve around the five community revitalization projects, which include Community Forums, Distinguished Grandmothers Ten Annual Portraits of Success, and Healthy Villages. Established in 1993, the organization is a strategic partner of United Way. As president of the entrustment, Ms. Williams-Curry has an extensive resume of service in public affairs and human relations. In her current position, she facilities the overall execution of the agency's goals and objectives and is responsible for all facets of financial management. Effectively marketing the organization's programs through public speaking engagements and fund-raising endeavors and by utilizing creative written and oral media presentations, Ms. Williams-Curry has made the entrustment a significant enterprise.

Career Steps: President, African-American Community Entrustment (1995–2000); Mediation and Communication, San Mateo County Government (1990–1995); KSOL-FM Radio, Public Affairs Director (1978–1990); Civil Law Investigator, San Mateo County Government (1975–1978); Human Relations Specialist, San Mateo Elementary School District (1966–1974).

Associations & Accomplishments: President, Bret Hart P.T.A./San Francisco; Peninsula Community Foundation;

Founder, Curry Fund for Low-Income Girls & Young Women (16–26 years old); San Francisco Foundation Award (1987); San Mateo County, Women's Hall of Fame Inductee (1994); Pilgrim Baptist Church, member serving in youth ministry; San Francisco Adult Day Health Network; Board Member of San Francisco Works; Bay Area Blacks in Philanthropy.

Education: Antioch College, B.A.in Human Relations and Creative Arts (1976).

Personal Information: Married to Richmond Earl Curry in 1946. They had eight children— Brenda, Bonnie, Barbara, Richmond Jr., James, William, Paul, and David—who have produced twenty-one grandchildren and five great-grandchildren. Mrs. Williams-Curry enjoys dancing, entertaining, reading, singing, sewing, walking, and writing.

You'll find in these pages my thoughts of life. It becomes apparent, as I confronted the challenges and made some hard necessary choices, that my life has not been easy. My life has been long. Thank God. Yes, it's been filled with hills and valleys. I've been called awful names, distasteful names, and unprintable names, but no one ever got away saying, "Girl, don't you know your place?"

CHAPTER ONE
1928–1933
MOTHER'S SMART, STRUGGLING SURVIVAL STYLE

It is a warm summer day, early May in St. Louis, Missouri. Mother has gone to work. Aunt Sally takes care of me until my big sister, Lois Mae comes from school.

"Child, here you done turned three years old. Some things you ought to know about yourself." Aunt Sally has long gray hair parted down the center and hanging straight past her chin. Her caramel-colored, wrinkled face with the little brown eyes looks at me. She seldom smiles, but her mouth is constantly in motion, telling us what we "ought to know."

"You were born in a house," she says. "No place for 'colored folks' over yonder." *Over yonder* is the white side of town. It seems like everything is over there except us. The main hospital is over there, reserved for "whites only."

"February 4, 1928, you was born," she grumbles. "Ophelia (my mother) gone and had another baby. Lord knows why—in the dead of freezing winter at that."

I look at her, curious.

"The Great Depression's still hanging 'round. It never left us. We manage to keep body and soul together. We help each other." She's talking to no one in particular, maybe to her three cats or the pigeons she keeps trying to catch.

I'm silent. *What is a great depression?* I think. I am trained to not talk, just listen.

"One of these days, you are going to understand what I'm telling you. St. Louis is the biggest city on the Mason-Dixon Line. The separation of coloreds and the whites is sure in this town. It seems like your mom doesn't know who she is or where she belongs. She got her education— I don't know for what. She's a trained nurse. Because of the crazy segregated laws, she can't even get a job at the hospital. Beats me."

"Aunt Sally, do you like Mama?" I ask, feeling that she is saying terrible things.

"Sure do," she replies. "You're too little for this stuff, but you need to know. Ophelia is too short for such big ideas. She is just four feet, eleven inches tall. She got that caramel-colored skin from Mama Thornton's side, with shoulder-length black hair. She goes everywhere with them two thick plaited braids. Your daddy! That man is six feet tall, with skin black as the top of your mama's kitchen stove. His skin is so black, it shines even without Vaseline." She laughs. "Your three uncles on your mother's side look like her too. All of them are light skinned. They hate your daddy and holler at your mother. They want to know why she married him. Our people know he's too dark to be hired for a decent-paying job. I know they either didn't holler loud enough or soon enough because it's five of you now. Listen, baby girl, don't tell anybody about our big talks, you hear me?" Aunt Sally likes to tell her tall tales.

"Yes, ma'am," I say, sitting on the bare porch steps next to Aunt Sally's rocking chair. We live on Fairfax Street in a big house with different families. Fairfax empties from the front door onto a dirt road. The other neighbors with real streets and sidewalks call us alley trash.

Where Is My Daddy?

Big people don't know it, but little kids like me hear so much when they talk. What they say does not make any sense because they explain nothing. I am three years old, trying to figure out what they are talking about. I wish I could ask them some questions when I think of stuff I need answers to.

Where is my daddy? I often think. What is his name? How come he never comes home? Lois Mae is older than me. She'd come home from school and say, "I'm going up to Daddy's."

"Can we go too?" Clifford would ask.

"No, just me. I have to get some money from him. I don't have time to be watching you." She would slam the bent-down screen door as she departed. She acted this way all the time.

This happened so much that I figured out my own answers: his name is Up-to-Daddy's. He lives on a job, where he can't come home. He has to stay all night and shovel coal in the furnace to keep the hotel rooms warm for the people living there. He works so Lois Mae can have money to help take care of us. When Up-to-Daddy's gives her money, she comes home skipping and smiling. She gets mad when he doesn't have any money.

I came up with another question. What is money?

Lois Mae goes straight to Mother.

"He's your husband!" Lois is shouting behind the closed bedroom door. "Why can't he come home?"

"Child, you're too young to understand or know," Mother whispers.

"Make me know!" Lois Mae demands.

"Keep your place." Mother is raising her voice.

I am standing close to the door. It's too quiet. I had better move away quickly. The door opens.

Shoot. I still don't know enough about Up-to-Daddy's.

I am four years old. It is warm outside, and I am crushing the leaves under my feet. Lois

Mae has to go see Up-to-Daddy's again, but this time she comes back too fast.

"Mother! Mother!" She is crying and screaming as she runs up the wooden steps.

"What happened?" Mother asks as she opens the door.

"It's Daddy!" Lois screams.

"What is it?" Mother is grabbing Lois's shoulders to calm her down. "What is it?"

"He's gone," Lois cries. They stand hugging each other, both silent. No one sees me. I am thinking. Gone where?

The next day and the next, people keep coming to our house from everywhere. They bring food, baskets of flowers, bags of fruit, and fried chicken wrapped in checkerboard tablecloths. I jump around, so happy. None of us can believe all that food—homemade cakes, jars of jelly, and homemade bread just for us.

People hug Mother, say hello to us kids, and leave. I like these people, but I don't know why they are here. I like them because they keep bringing food.

Two days later, we get up early and put on our Sunday "go-to-meeting" clothes. These clothes are usually saved for Sunday, but today is Saturday. I am still so happy that I start clapping my hands, dancing and singing.

"Stop prancing around," Charles, one of my older brothers, says as he frowns at me. "You are giving the wrong impression."

"What's impression?" I ask.

"Just shut up and watch," he replies.

Next, my uncles start showing up. Uncle Cecil, the saxophone player and the only one with an old Model T Ford, has his Sunday clothes on too. I am puzzled. He has on a black suit, white shirt, a black tie, and patent leather shoes. Next, I see Uncle King Bob and Uncle Woody. Everybody is dressed up. Charles lifts me into the Model T to sit next to Mother because I'm the smallest. We drive off.

We stop at the church and get out. As we walk inside to take our seats, I think. Why are we here? It is quiet. The preacher goes to the front, and I see a long, closed box sitting in the center up front. The choir sings, and the preacher talks about the person in the box, not calling any name I know.

"Who's in that box?" I ask Mother.

"Be quiet," she whispers. "I'll tell you later."

By the end of the service, I figure it out. Daddy's gone. But where did he go? Nobody ever said where he went. Lois Mae stopped going 'up-to-Daddy's.

"Your daddy is in heaven," Aunt Sally tells me during one of our private talks. I am four years old.

"Where is heaven?" I ask.

"One day, you will understand. Now hush." I wonder if this is another of her tall tales.

Curry Spice: If people tell tall tales on you, they must have nothing else to do.

CHAPTER TWO
1934–1939
Valuable Lessons of Life

Kindergarten—One Day Only

"I'm going to keep you with me and teach you how to read," Mother says, smiling.

I am five years old, and I smile back at her, thinking, I'm going to have her all to myself. She loves me. I didn't know the true reason until months later when Lois Mae, my oldest sister, said, "Mother kept you home because she didn't have enough money to buy you any shoes. Who cares if you can read? You're already a year behind." I felt sad and listened helplessly. I decided Lois was too bossy.

I am six years old, and I start kindergarten today. At the end of the day, the teacher pins a note on my blouse to take to Mother. I take the note off and read it out loud. The teacher comes over to me and asks, "Who taught you to read?"

"My mother," I whisper proudly. The teacher wants me to bring Mother to school tomorrow.

The next day, Mother comes to school with me. The teacher and principal decide I should be moved to the first grade.

Hospital Sign: For Whites Only

I am eight years old, and on that spring day, my brothers and their friends are playing baseball with a homemade broomstick, using cork soda-bottle tops as a ball. Girls can watch, not play. However, I run into the playing field.

"Look out!" someone yells.

I duck down, but the broomstick grazes my face just beneath my left eye. My brother Clifford rushes over and grabs me close. He says he doesn't see any blood. "Stay out of the way," he whispers, and the game starts again.

Two weeks later, Mother notices that my head is leaning to the left. She holds my face with both hands, staring at me.

"What's going on with your left eye?" she asks. The rest of the week, she checks my eye repeatedly. It isn't looking straight ahead and won't move.

Clifford watches her. "What's wrong, Mama?" he asks. Remembering the stickball game, he says, "Maybe it happened when Eleanor almost ran into the broomstick bat last week."

Mother tells Aunt Sally that she's taking me to the hospital where the signs say "For Whites Only." She believes I need an eye operation. We are the talk of our few little blocks. Anything out of the daily routine creates big excitement among our nosy neighbors:

"Ophelia is beside herself again."
"They tell me the white folks at the hospital are arguing about the operation for her little girl."
"Yeah, Ophelia ought to know better than to think it can happen."
"She is stirring up a heap of trouble. Might be bad for some of us if they think we sent her over there."

"Everywhere you go there are signs saying 'For Whites Only' and 'No Coloreds Allowed.'"
"Who she does think she is? Miss In-between?" The group falls out laughing.
"I ain't never seen no signs saying, 'For In-Betweens only." The laughter grows louder.

I am scared, but I think Mother can fix any problem I have. Days pass, and soon there is more talk from the neighbors. I see concerned looks and hear hushed voices, especially when I go to school. The kids pretend not to see me.

The neighbors start anew:

"What if Ophelia gets us in hot water because we know her?" They whisper, sounding scared.
"They made Ophelia get out of that front office. She knows better than to walk past them signs."
"I heard she took poor little Eleanor with her."
"Ophelia thinks that if they see the child, they'll let her through the door. I bet they get kicked out. Good thing it's warm."
"Wonder what's going to happen. If Ophelia doesn't get out, they could haul her and the child off to jail."

Mother picks me up early from school, and she's smiling. "We won, baby. We're ready to get your eye straight. But you keep it a secret until it's all over." She bends over and hugs me.

"What happened?" I ask.

"Remember the doctor from up North who said hello to you? He fixed everything. I'll tell you on the way home. Let's go catch our bus."

I am happy as we get on the bus. I rest my head on Mother's shoulder, dropping off to sleep. Next thing I know, we are home.

Aunt Sally is waiting on our porch. "What happened over yonder, Ophelia?" she asks. "Better be careful, honey, you could get yourself and that child killed. Know what I mean? That child can see. Better to have a weak eye than to be gone forever."

Mother unlocks the door as Aunt Sally waits with a sad look.

"Come on in. Get that doomsday, worried look off your face," Mother says with a smile. "A new doctor from up North came into that big office the other day when a clerk was kicking us out. This doctor is the best and brightest of the current staff. He entered the main waiting room as we were being forced to leave. He smiled at Eleanor, came closer asking her what her name is.

"The clerk shouted at the doctor about no coloreds being allowed into this hospital. The clerk is agitated, turning his attention to me, and he comes from behind his desk pointing his finger, telling me to get out before he calls the police to lock me up.

"The doctor didn't know what was happening. He had just witnessed the crazy law of segregation in the raw. He almost raised both hands to stop the outburst. Instead, he looked toward the exit, making a motion for me to go outside now.

"Honey, five minutes later he came outside and checked Eleanor's eyes right there. He confirmed that an operation was necessary. I was baffled, thinking it won't be done in that hospital. He promised he'd call for me to return, and he did. A month later, I went back. You won't believe what he told me!" Mother gets excited.

"He'd been told he could not operate on the child's eye because coloreds were not allowed in the "Whites Only" hospital. He threatened to resign. Things were stalled for almost two weeks. In desperation, he pleaded with the top administrators, sharing his oath to save any person. He told them she's just a little girl and that moral values are above man-made laws. They still told the doctor no way. Guess what he decided to do? He announced to the hospital folks that he operates or he leaves. The administrators were shocked and reluctantly agreed. Praise the Lord!" Mother cries.

Aunt Sally grins, eager to go tell our nosy neighbors. "Wait," Mother whispers. "This has to remain a secret until the operation is over." Mother wipes her eyes on the back of her sleeve. "You promise not to say a word?" Aunt Sally agrees. The next week, Mother takes me back to the hospital, and a half day later, it's over. The operation is a success.

A Fourth-Grade Teacher

Two weeks later, at eight thirty in the morning, I return to school with a big white bandage held onto my forehead and cheek with slabs of plastic tape. The rest of my face can barely be seen. The kids laugh and holler, dancing around me.

"Hey!" they shout. "Here's the one-eyed monster, the one-eyed monster, the one-eyed monster!"

I am terrified. As the kids get louder and louder, I'm wishing the building would swallow me up for protection. The bell rings.

"Boys and girls. Get in line immediately," a voice says. I see Miss Delaney, our fourth-grade teacher. I thought, my angel! We enter our classroom—no talk of geography, timetables, or good manners today. It's so quiet that we can hear an eraser moving across a piece of paper.

"Boys and girls, we have a very important, special lesson to learn today." Miss Delaney is deliberate, determined, and distressed. "We must always help when someone is hurt or in pain or having a difficult time. Do you understand?"

"Yes, ma'am," a chorus of thirty-seven voices replies.

"Your classmate Eleanor recently had a serious eye operation. She is four weeks behind in her lessons. What can each of you do to help her catch up? Now be quiet and think of the best thing to do. Tell me after recess."

Miss Delaney keeps track of my progress until I finish the back lessons, sometimes staying after class. "I am impressed with your progress," she says. Miss Delaney is a stern yet fair teacher. "Eleanor, you are going to be a credit to our race one day." She says, holding both of my hands, looking keen and serious.

"Thank you, Miss Delaney," I say while thinking. A credit to our race! What does that mean?

Curry Spice: Be cool; have no fear. Good help is always near.

CHAPTER THREE
1940–1945
MOTHER'S FAMILY WISDOM

DID CLIFFORD JOIN THE ARMY?

Clifford is five feet, nine inches tall; has a spicy brown skin tone; and is lean and gentle. He is twenty-one years old, six years older than I am, and he can't find a job in St. Louis due to the separation laws. He lives as a hobo or works as a migratory worker to get away from the southern states. He catches a train leaving St. Louis and going to Chicago, and Mother waits to hear if he has reached Chicago.

Guess how he ends up in New York? When the train stops in the middle of the country, he is sound asleep. The train moves on, and he wakes up in New York. When he arrives, he takes the few coins he managed to save and calls Mother.

"Hello, Mom," he begins. "I'm doing fine. I'm staying with a guy I met on the train. I'll look for work tomorrow. Oh. I forgot to mention—I ended up in New York." Clifford waits for Mother to say something.

"How in the world did you make it completely across the country?" she asks, sounding shocked.

"Don't get excited, Mom," Clifford replies. He is running out of money. "I'll be in touch. Love you. Bye."

Three weeks pass without any more word from Clifford. Mother prays early in the morning and late into the night, asking God to keep Clifford safe from danger in that big city where he has no money.

Still without a job and getting desperate, he calls. "Hello, Mom."

"I'm so glad to hear your voice," Mother says. Her voice firm and full of concern, she rushes on. "I sense you still are not working. I don't want you to end up in jail. Please join the army today."

"What army?" Clifford says, bewildered. "The army is not for us. It's still segregated."

"Join the army, segregated or not." Mother raises her voice. "You must do it now! Yes! Today! You have three younger brothers following in your footsteps. If you start stealing just to feed yourself, they'll do the same. Promise me you'll do it today."

"I have to go, Mom," Clifford says quickly. "I'll check out the army deal just for you. Bye."

Mother receives a postcard one month later from Clifford: "I'm in the army now," it says.

Where Can I Get a Job?

I am fourteen years old. Only Mother, my twelve-year-old brother, and I live at home, in one of the buildings called "the Flats." There are twenty to thirty buildings in the Flats, with four flats to each section, two up and two down. Each flat consists of two rooms—a kitchen and an oversized bedroom. Each building has only one toilet and one tub, so the four resident families share these facilities. Mother prepares to bathe me by heating a bucket of water on the kitchen stove and pouring the water into a large number three tin tub. We have no electricity, only candles and cold kerosene lamps. These are probably the cheapest housing units in the whole city, and I am not allowed to go out after dark. A large, uncovered garbage dump is out in the backyard, where big, gray rats stay invisible during the day but take over at night. I hate living in this nightmare building.

I realize the hardships Mother endures. She can barely pay the meager rent, so forget feeding us two teenagers three square meals a day. I generally pretend that everything is going great when I'm in the outside world; I even made straight A's in the beginning of high school. But internally, I am terrified that I might not survive, yet I know I must stay alive. Today I decide to change this poverty-stricken life. I can no longer live this dual life. I need a job. God knows we need the money. I decide I'll work in the tavern near our house. No way, Mother declares. She works as a maid, and I try to figure out how to tell her I will not work as a maid.

She finds me a part-time job on the "white side of town." It is at a resort hotel, which includes a restaurant for its customers. I am a new bus girl, and I am thrilled. Mother's new directive to me is, "If your grades happen to get lower, the job will be gone."

I maintain good grades. In fact, I make A's in every subject right up to my sophomore year. My principal was so excited about my flawless record that he contacted the Missouri State Department of Education and requested that an official come and review my records. If the official approved of them, that meant I would get a four-year college scholarship at the university. Mother and I can't believe our ears when my principal tells us what could happen. Shortly, a white gentleman comes to see us and says, "I have to interview you to record some of your family history as we proceed."

"Fine," Mother says. "I work pretty hard to raise my children. Eleanor is the last one at home with me."

Today is Monday, the day we'll find out if I qualify for the scholarship, and I am too eager to get to school to wait for Mother to join me. Once at school, I go to the principal's outer office and sit down to relax. I hear loud voices coming from inside his office, and I recognize one of them as the principal's: "I'm telling you, she is that smart! It's not just the academics. She is emotionally balanced and good in sports. I know she can succeed in college. She can handle college!"

"I disagree with you," the other voice, belonging to the state official, says. He raises his voice. "I stayed with this through the weekend, reviewing the entirety of her records. This is an aberration. It's a fluke."

"You are dead wrong!" The principal is getting heated. "You have not convinced me with one solid grain of evidence to support your findings." I sat there surprised, stilled, and stunned. They are discussing me, I thought.

"Here's the best damn reason of all," the state official says, rushing out his final words. "Her father was just a janitor before he died, and her mother is a lowly maid."

I am in shock—yes, shock. I run from the office, race back home, regain my composure, and go inside, determined not to upset Mother.

"Mother," I say, "you don't have to go to the school after all. I don't want to go to college."

"What happened?" she asked. She knew something had gone wrong. "Are you all right?"

"Sure. I might not be college material," I say. "I'll try college later." I feel the tears welling up in my eyes. "I've got to go back to school." I make it to the bus stop and then cry for fifteen minutes before the next bus arrives.

Mother's Main Issue

Two years later, Mother's health is not good. She is overweight, and her doctor tells her to lose eighty pounds. I don't really know what is ailing Mother because Aunt Sally will not talk about her health and none of the neighbors ever discuss being sick, either.

October, my favorite time of year, is extra warm. Gold, reddish brown and yellow leaves pile in small heaps in the gutter and drift across the sidewalks. I walk, crushing the leaves underfoot, and break out in a hot sweat. That's odd, I think. The day is not hot enough to sweat. Something is wrong with Mother! I start running. It's a good thing I run on the track team. Six blocks later, I'm home. Pushing open the door, I see Aunt Sally standing by Mother, who is lying on the couch, her face drawn, unable to smile. "You made it," she whispers. I freeze in the doorway.

"Wait!" I say. "I'll run and get the doctor." My voice is hushed and shouting at the same time. The doctor's office is two blocks away, so soon I'm running again. I push open his door, and he smiles.

"It's Mother!" I say, breathless.

"Eleanor," Dr. Levin says, focusing on me, "what's wrong with your mom?"

"She doesn't look good," I say. "She hasn't been eating. I'm scared."

"Let's go!" Dr. Levin jumps up, grabs his black bag, pulls out his car keys, and we're on our way. It seems like just sixty seconds before we're there. I open the door, peering to the spot where Mother lies on the couch. But it's too late. Aunt Sally pulls the sheet over Mother's head, not uttering a word. I am dumbfounded.

Death news travels fast. Very soon, the entire neighborhood knows Mother has died. I am devastated. "Why?" I ask.

Mother was a woman of many moods. She must have had a hard time raising her six children by herself after Daddy died. At that time, Lois Mae was only twelve years old, Clifford was ten, Charles was eight, Roy was six, I was four, and Earl Kenneth was two.

Mother was too tired to keep going. She was the center of my life.

I remember how she crocheted doilies and bedspreads to brighten our small house. She knew how to sew and knit. She was a splendid cook, preserving and canning foods for us to eat during the winter. She was also a proficient reader and loved to sing. She was cheerful, had a keen sense of humor, and kept a positive attitude. She insisted that her children be able to think for themselves.

She made us siblings attend any church near our house, and she wanted us to be properly educated. Also, her house had to be quiet, and no cursing was ever allowed. Mother also made precise decisions when necessary.

One afternoon when Dad returned from work, he seemed angry.

"Ophelia, come here," he said. "Did you finish washing and ironing my seven white shirts today?"

"Of course," Mother answered, thinking of the iron she had to heat on the kitchen stove. She had to be careful not to burn the shirts. "What's the matter?"

"There's too much starch in the last bunch." Dad was very annoyed. "I'll have to teach you a lesson you'll never forget." He took the shirts she had ironed, carried them to the bathtub, ran cold water in it, and dumped the shirts in the water, hollering, "Ophelia, do you think you can put the right amount of starch in my shirts next time?"

Mother stood still, her face deadpan, not saying one word.

"I have to work late tonight," Dad said as he walked out, slamming the front door.

"Hello, King Bob," Mother says a few moments later, talking to her oldest brother on the phone. "I need you to come over to change the lock on my front door. Roy doesn't live here anymore."

Mother also had a sense of humor, and she tried to pass it on to her children. "These kids of mine are either going to be natural-born comedians or darn fools," she said, talking to a friend who had moved to Chicago. A year later, they talked again, and the friend asked, "How are the kids?"

"Well," Mother replied, "none of them have turned into natural-born comedians yet."

She also insisted that her children be able "to think." The next story is an example of what she considered "thinking."

And Mother Said to Me

"You talked to Helen on the phone about going to the new bowling alley tonight," Mother says. "Don't go. It's too dangerous."

"Mother, there are four of us," I protest stubbornly. "What can possibly happen?"

"One of you could get shot," she replies. "That's it. Don't go."

"All right, Mother." I normally obey Mother, but I'm thinking, Nothing will happen. Helen, Thelma, and Arlene meet me at the bus stop as planned and reveal that their moms had said no too. We discuss whether we should go to the movies or the bowling alley. The bowling alley it is.

We climb aboard the bus, happy, laughing, and undaunted. We are up for some Friday night fun, and the intersection of Finney and Sarah Streets is the hottest spot in St. Louis. We get our tickets, and the walkways are full of people. We have to wait fifteen minutes for a lane to become available. After just one set, we hear a loud firecracker … and then another. We panic as gunshots ring out—boom, boom, boom. People are screaming, scrambling, and shoving. Mother's voice rings in my ears: "Don't go." I drop the bowling ball and look for my three friends, but they are nowhere in sight.

"Oh, my God," I say to myself. "Where did they go?" Police sirens are wailing in my ears. I squeeze down the aisle through the scramble of people until I'm outside in the back alley. I cross the open lot to Finney Street and see that all the streets are overflowing with people who are pushing, trying to get on the buses. I am just six blocks from home, so I decide to run. I completely forget about my friends until I see the long sidewalk up to my house.

I pause, free from the chaos and trying to collect my racing thoughts. Things appear normal. Darkness dominates the night. Stars are shining. The moon is clear. A few lights are visible among the mostly darkened houses. It is spooky and quiet, except for my thumping heart, but I am home. Mother hears my key in the door.

"Oh, the movie is over early," Mother says with a smile. "What did you see? Is that clock right? It has 9:35 p.m."

"I'm a little tired," I mumble. "Can we talk in the morning?" I'm moving as slowly and as quickly as I dare.

"Sure, baby," she says. "You're working too hard."

"Good night," I say without giving a hint of the bowling alley scene. I get no sleep that night—more like a nightmare. Do I tell Mother or not?

"Don't worry 'til worry worries you," she often says to me. What happened to my friends? I can't sleep. Finally, daylight peeks through the thin curtain; Saturday is here already. I stay in bed until noon when a faint knock at the door wakes me up. Who in the world …? I jump out of bed, grab my robe, and splash water on my face. Mother is already opening the door.

"Good morning, Helen!" she says. "What brings you out so early on a Saturday morning?"

"Hi Mrs.Williams." Helen sounds devious. "Is Eleanor here?"

"What time is it?" I ask, appearing in the kitchen. I can't believe Helen is here. "Are you all right?" I ask. She is too calm for my taste. "Are you going somewhere?"

"Oh, not now, I might shop tomorrow." She also sounds too sweet.

"What time did you get home from the bowling alley?" she asks. "Did you run into any trouble? Was your mother upset with you for going?" She is staring at me.

Stone silence. I feel like Joe Louis has delivered me his famous knockout punch. I feel angry, betrayed, and speechless. Mother is watching this exchange. Breathless, I want to slap Helen. Instead, I stand frozen, glaring at her. I hear voices.

"Well, now, Helen," Mother begins, obviously in charge. "Tell me the rest of what happened since you want to talk."

"I thought Eleanor told you," Helen says, but she knows better. "We didn't mean to do it. It was awful. The police found me under the stairwell. They brought me home. Mother was furious. Are you mad at Eleanor, too?" Helen's voice is high-pitched, fading, rising, and whispering. "I am so upset, and …" She starts to cry.

"Hush, child," Mother says. "You'd better go home now."

"Please don't beat Eleanor," Helen says. "I can't go anywhere for a month." She's still crying.

"Dry your eyes and go home," Mother says.

Helen glances at me with a pitiful face, and I am feeling sorry for her. Can you believe it?

"Well, honey," Mother begins. "What did you learn from Helen with that outburst?" She waits for an answer.

"Mother, I'm so sorry. I feel terrible."

"Spare me the pity," she replies. "Stop whining. You punished yourself during the night. I heard you toss and turn without knowing what was bothering you."

I cannot believe my ears.

"So, what did you learn about a friend like Helen? Your only punishment is to stay away from her for a while. By the way, look up the word squealer."

Mother always wanted me to finish high school and go to college. She made me save money every week from my meager salary—ten dollars a week, plus tips. This was an order. When she died, she did not have any insurance. I had saved 423 dollars, and I used it to bury her. No college, but I love my mother.

Curry Spice: Wisdom is brainpower—ready for whoever needs it, no matter the hour.

CHAPTER FOUR
1946–1951
READY OR NOT, CHANGES COME

GRADUATION MILESTONE

In January 1946, Uncle Cecil bought me a new winter coat for a graduation present. The principal sent a letter stating the following: "Eleanor Williams is a new member of the Honor Society, having completed her major academics in three and half years. She is one of the top ten graduates [of the] Class of 1946."

This news eases the tension I feel as a result of being an orphan, no longer having a job, and wondering how I'll pay the rent. What can I do?

My thoughts flash back to Richmond Earl Curry, the captain of the football team. Everybody knows him, even beyond the Sumner High School area, except me. I am on the track team, and I know nothing of football. It is late September, a perfect, warm, and sunny afternoon. I'm dressed in all white, including my running shorts. I didn't know Richmond was practicing football with his players on the inner field.

"Who is that?" Richmond asks with a keen interest.

"That's Eleanor Williams, man." Ernest answers. "You can forget her. She's my neighbor. All she does is study, run track, and work part-time." He laughs as the master of authority.

"I want to meet her," Richmond says, persistent.

"All right, man, but you're wasting your time. I'll introduce you. But I bet you ten bucks you won't get to first base with her."

"That's a deal. When I win, don't go near her anymore. Al right?"

"Hey man, this will be the easiest ten bucks I ever made," Ernest replies. "You are wasting your time. She does not date, man. But come on, let's go."

They both run over to me, and I turn to see who is coming so close.

"Hello, Eleanor," Ernest says. "Someone wants to meet you. This is Richmond Earl Curry." Ernest bows, extending his hand toward Richmond.

"Hello," we both say almost at once. Then we stand in an awkward silence that seems to last for hours.

"Nice meeting you," I say. "See you around." I start running again, thinking he's too quiet.

Over the next several weeks, Richmond pops up in my life during school at the most unexpected moments.

"I'll see you after the break," he says. "But call me Earl like everybody else does." He constantly returns, always friendly, always smiling. It is getting harder and harder to hold him at bay. He is an amazing, incredible, handsome teenager.

"What can I do for you today, Earl?" I ask. He has appeared two days in a row.

"You can lend me a quarter. I promise to pay you back." He has broken the ice. I laugh as I hand him a quarter. The next day, he returns.

"Your quarter turned into fifty cents," he says, handing me two quarters. "I can't stay today." He continues to appear and pull his crazy antics with a contagious smile that begins to penetrate my dreams.

In early November, before Mother got sick, I invite Earl to meet her. She likes him in an instant and allows us to see each other. We are courting in fewer than six months. We go to the movies, to dances, to dinner, to the bowling alley, to the outdoor opera, and to football games. I do not understand football, but I enjoy being with Earl.

"Why did you want to see me so much?" I ask on one of our dates.

"When we first met, I was appalled that you didn't know me," he answers. "I told Ernest that same day, 'I'm going to marry her so she shall never forget me.'" We both laugh.

The more time we spend together, the more convinced I become that we are in love. We both keep our grades high and keep our part-time jobs. We are teenage sweethearts. Earl is a senior and is accepted to Kentucky State College, which means he is leaving at the end of the summer in 1945. I wonder what I'll do when he goes to college. I graduate with honors from Sumner High School in St. Louis, Missouri, in January 1946. I certainly am not prepared for how fast my life would change over the rest of that year.

What Is Marriage?

Once Mother passed, in 1945, Earl cannot stand my facing terrible situations alone. He sends letters from college and sometimes calls.

"I'm coming home immediately to marry you," Earl says emphatically on the telephone. "I'll be home for Christmas."

"Wait. I'm graduating in January," I state. "You still have two more years of college."

"You're more important," he replies. "You know I love you. Be careful until I get home."

My family is in the military and scattered about. Some of my family lives in Chicago. But most of Earl's family lives in St. Louis. They embrace me. We are married in the spacious living room of Earl's parents' home.

Rev. Mitchell reads our marriage vows, from the King James Version of the Bible, to us. He says, "A man shall leave his father and mother and be joined unto his wife, and they shall be one flesh, and cling together for better or worse 'til death do them part, forsaking all others as long as they both shall live."

Our first living quarters is one bedroom in the house of Earl's elderly cousin, Emma, where we share the kitchen. Earl finds an apartment in four months, which we share with Samuel, his younger brother, and Peggy, his new wife. I discover more of the Curry family.

Watson and Nellie Curry have ten children: three older girls and seven boys. Their names are Alice Adell, Ruth, Rosa, Watson Jr. (Sonny), James Arnold, Richmond Earl, Samuel, Rupert, Travers, and Michael Leonard. They were trained to look out for one another, as well as any in-laws. When I needed to learn something, one of the family members would me, and then , teach me too. Guess what I had to learn? I did not know how to cook. So, Ruth, the second sister, took charge of my daytime life for four weeks, teaching me as she went. And now, I can cook!

Getting adjusted to being married is full of surprises. We are passionate with each other, having three baby daughters only thirteen months apart. Two years pass, and then we have two sons in the next two years. Talk about life changing. Our devotion to each other and our five kids becomes overwhelming to me most times. My main tasks are to care for the kids, keep the house clean, handle grocery shopping, have dinner ready every day, and pay the bills—always pay the bills! There is not ever enough money to reach to the end of the month.

I become a superb cook through all of this. Earl comes home from work, and the aroma from the apple cobbler flows to his nostrils.

"Hello, Sweetheart," he says. "I love you more when you cook." He hugs me. "I just thought of something you don't do. You never ask me to make love to you."

"You never give me a chance," I say, very surprised. He stands there for a few minutes. I'm not sure why. "Are you ready for your dinner?"

"Does that mean you're putting me on hold?" he asks with a smile, and I laugh. "I'll call you back later," he says.

Although the southern states are still very segregated, Earl has a new job at the major "colored Deluxe Hotel" owned by Charles Abernathy, the colored real estate dealer, and his wife, Rosa. Fortunately, Rosa is Earl's sister. The Deluxe Hotel is the hub of the colored neighborhood since they hire many of our people. Anyone who wants to work is trained to do a job. All the major sports celebrities and national entertainers stay at the Deluxe Hotel when traveling, due to the separation laws.

Curry Spice: Separate laws and money too short, so love is the main part.

CHAPTER FIVE
1952–1957
Segregation Is Too Severe

Money Challenges

When the Jim Crow laws relaxed to a small degree, within months of Jackie Robinson becoming the first black baseball player in the major leagues, the white hotels opened their doors. This caused an exodus to the other side of town, crippling businesses on the colored side of town. Earl goes back to parking cars at the major shopping center, but the salary is still not enough to care for the seven of us.

A problem comes up at work. Management wants to extend the hours of all the colored workers without giving overtime pay, yet the white workers would receive more pay for the extra work. Earl refuses to go along with the new plan. He believes everyone should be treated equally. The other colored workers decide that Earl is a troublemaker and report him as such to top management. His brother mentions the conflict to me, but I hesitate to let Earl know that I have this information.

Migrating to Another State

One Wednesday evening, he comes home tired yet in a happy mood. As we finish dinner, he says, "What do you think about moving to California?"

"Where is California?" I ask. "When will this happen?" I think. He is losing his mind.

"That's where Alice lives," he explains, referring to his oldest sister. "She will let me stay with her until I get a job."

"What about me and the kids?"

"I'll send for you right away, like maybe six months," he says.

"When are you leaving?"

"Hey, baby. That means yes. I'm ready to go!"

"When?" I ask again, nervous.

"I'll be ready this weekend."

Earl has a brand new aqua-colored station wagon, which he gasses up and loads with a picnic basket, heading for a new destination. He drives for three days and two nights over more than two thousand miles. "I made it. Thank God," he says. He joins the Carpenters Union and starts saving money to send to us.

Curry Spice: Change places someday. You will be moving ahead another way.

Ophelia Thornton-Williams, Regisrtered Nurse, mother of
six children. Lives in St. Louis, Missouri (1940)

Earl Kenneth Williams, youngest son of Ophelia Williams,
living in St. Louis, Missouri. (1948)

Richmond Earl Curry, Captain of Sumner High Schhol, Football Team. St. Louis, Missouri 1943-1945

Eleanor Williams. Track team member, Senior Choir Student at Sumner High Schhol. St. Louis. Missouri..

Eleanor and Earl enjoy an evevning out after 35 yeers of marriage , now living in San Mateo,California, (1976)

Eleanor Williams. Sumner High School. Honor Society, one of top ten students graduates Class of 1946. St. Louis,

Eleanor, President of Bret Harte P.T.A., with student, Henry morris. Pacific Bell and Joe Bailey, United Crusade at Alice Griffin Hoiusing Project. San Francisco, CA. (1963)

Richmond Earl and Eleanor Curry, with their eight children, members of Bayview Luthern Church, where they are all baptised, in Hunter's Point, San Francisco, California. (1961)

From the left; Paul 6, William (Bill) 8, Mama holding David, 4, on Grafton Avenue in San Francisco, California. 1964)

Eleanor, Erma Prothro and Claire Mack have been close friends for 45 years. They graduated from Antioch College together in 1976. Erma is a Practicing Psychologist. Claire is the first African American Mayor of San Mateo, California.

Portait of Eleanor, Public Affairs Director, KSOL-Radio, San Mateo, California, celebrating its Halloween party , 1980.

Ana Navarro, Director of Mediation, San Mateo County Government with Eleanor. Ana works directly with the Court Department and District Attorney. She is a Diversity Trainer. Together the women served offering Diversity Training to approxi...

Janet Frakes, First Director of the Advisory Counil on Women for San Mateo County Government with Eleanor during the Work Plans on Women's issues. Janet is an excellent communicator keeping the volunteers energized and on target. The Women's...

ELEANOR CURRY

Advisory Council of Women Charter Member Commissioners San Mateo County. First row left is Janet Frakes, First Director, June 1985. San Mateo County, Redwood City, California. Established November, 1982

Honoring Eleanor Curry, third from left with other recipients, receiving "ABE LINCOLN MERIT AWARD"SOUTHERN BAPTIST RADIO-TELEVISION COMMISSION", Houston, Texas, February 11, 1982

ELEANOR CURRY

From left, Eleanor with Anita Webb, Coordinator of MLK. Jr. Essay and Poetry Contest, Kindergarten to High School students, Dr. Emmette Carson, President & CEO, Silicon Valley Community Foundation, Mountain View, Keynote speaker and Ethel Burnside, President of North Central Neighborhood Association and producer of the MLK.Jr. Essay and Poetry contest, held annually, at the Community Center in San Mateo, California. (2008)

From left, Claire Mack, first African-American Mayor of the City of San Mateo, Eleanor, Dennis Caines, African American Attorney and Mindy Pengilly, Real Estate Services. attending San Mateo Public Library Awards Event in San Mateo, California (2007)

Eleanor and Richmond Earl Curry renewing their marriage vows with Mrs. Jackie Speier, AssemblyMember. officiating with the Currys and thier immediate family relatives. (1994)

Eleanor with Jill Wakeman, Founder OF FOUNDATION FOR EQUALITY. go to www.CupsForEquality.org for more details and to donate. The Curry Fund for Girls and Young Women (16-26) is one of the recipients . Cups for equality philosophy is "Give a Cup. Change a Life."

Marlene Jones-Schoonover, Healthy Villages, Project
Director with Sheila Hill-Fajors at "An Evening Reception"

Angela, Diane and Eleanor, three key United Way staff
members discussing programs for students for nine

Will Spencer, an important fund-raising Administrator, giving
Eleanor critical tips and solid principles. (i998)

Daniel with his adopted son, Patrick. Barry Bonds, United
Way Board member and Eleanor, enjoying Sheila's

President Thomas Ruppanner, of the United Way of the Bay Area, San Francisco, California. (1985 -2005)

Dick Rosenberg, Leader of Bank of America and Chairman of the United Way during Tom;s tenure.

Eleanor receives the 'Olympic Torch' for developing and strengthing the minds of students meeting with three of her young students. (1994) (1994)

ELEANOR CURRY

Family Portrait at Family Reunion in San Mateo, CA. From left bottom seating order, James Arnold, Paul, William (Bill), anr Richmond, Jr. Standing back row, Barbara, Bonnie, Papa Curry, David, Mama Curry and Brenda. Photo by Sears Photo Shop. Hillsdale, San Mateo (2005)

From left, Bernie Moody, K-WAV-Radio, Monterey, California, Eleanor, hostess and Eva Rhodes, Community Activist celebrating Eva's birthday in San Carlos, California. (2007)

Rev.Clifford Williams, now retired, is a Chaplain at local prisons, Chicago,Illinois, with his younger sister, Eleanor, on vacation together at his home (2005)

From the left, Lenneal Henderson, Jr., Marcella Henderson, retired LVN and matriarch of the family, Carolyn, Mark, Savon and in front, Linda, family historian and communicator. (2010)

Third from left, Marcella Henderson with three generations of the Henderson families.

CHAPTER SIX
1958–1963
Northern Freedom

Who Is a Good Neighbor?

Lenneal Henderson, born in Sand Hill, Mississippi, served his country during World War II as a Sergeant First Class in the US Army. He moved to New Orleans, where he met his wife, Marcella, and then went to San Francisco to seek a better life for his wife and children. Lenneal is a man of immense courage, immense genius, and immense love. Earl and I met the Henderson family when we moved to Hunters Point (the Hill) in San Francisco in 1955.

"Hello, we are the Henderson!" Lenneal, an accomplished electronics mechanic, and Marcella, a nurse at the local hospital, greeted us when we arrived. "We have six children," Lenneal says. "I hear you have seven. Are you Catholic?"

"No, man," Earl says. "My dad has ten kids. I decided I wanted to be like him."

"Forget being like your dad. Didn't you learn from him how hard it is to feed ten people every single day? Don't even think about a vacation. Come over anytime except for dinner." They smile and shake our hands. We are new neighbors.

Lenneal has a robust sense of humor.

"Marcella can cut a chicken into twenty-one pieces. With eight of us eating, that's enough to go around with a couple of pieces still on the plate." Lenneal is talking of how swift kids are when food is too good. "I taught these kids to never eat the last piece of food. I want this chicken, and I wish they would leave so I won't seem greedy. One of them drops a fork near me, so I bend down to pick it up and straighten back up. The last piece of chicken is gone. I'm flabbergasted. 'All of you can go to your room now,' I said. The next Sunday, the same thing happened, but I'm ready this time. Somebody dropped a fork, and I reached over, stuck my fork in the piece of chicken, and then reached down to retrieve the fork."

"Lenneal, you are so funny," I say. "You should try to do comedy at the Hungry I Club in San Francisco."

"Are you kidding me? I have enough hungry eyes watching me now."

Carolyn, the Henderson's twelve-year-old daughter, is the chief dishwasher. Carolyn knocks at our back door with the big pot I had given to Marcella the night before, which was filled with Chicken and dumplings. This morning the pot is empty and unwashed.

"Mama said thank you for the food," Carolyn says. "Here's your pot, Mrs. Curry. "I have enough dishes and pans to wash, so I thought you could wash your own pots." Her dad made her take the pot back and wash it.

Linda, the ten-year-old daughter, is nicknamed The Negotiator. On Thanksgiving Day, both of our families have the kids write brief paragraphs on the topic "I am thankful for…" Linda wins with this: "I am thankful for having a good family. I am thankful for my daddy, who sometimes has to spank us so we can act better. He tells us the spanking is going to hurt him more than us. I think Daddy has that part wrong, but I'm not going to tell him yet."

Savon, the Henderson's three-year-old daughter, regularly shocks her mother. "Eleanor," Marcella begins, "I don't know what I'm going to do with Savon. I get off at seven in the morning. By the time I get home, I am bone-tired. When I put her to bed next to me, trying to get her to sleep, she begins to cry. You cannot imagine what she did the next day."

"What did she do?"

"When I closed my eyes, she got right in front of me and opened my eyelids, saying, 'I not sleepy. I take nap already. Go to sleep, Mommy.' What am I going to do?"

I laugh at Marcella's exhausted expression. "Bring her over here. Savon is right. Your daughters put her to bed at eight o'clock every night. I'll keep her until you get up in the afternoon."

Marcella was born in New Orleans in 1924, when Calvin Coolidge was president. The economy was booming, a loaf of bread cost six cents, and gasoline was eight cents a gallon. While working as a waitress at the old Roosevelt Hotel (now the Fairmont Hotel) in New Orleans, she not only met Lenneal Henderson but also received a big tip from Robert Taylor, the famous actor.

Once Marcella and I become close friends, I ask her how to start working for a salary.

"I need a job to help out," I explain, "but Earl does not want me to work. Do you have any thoughts?"

"Girl, go get yourself a job," she advised. "He'll be toasting you with champagne in less than six months. Mark my word!"

Although the Henderson family often made us laugh, their courage made them effective in both the church and the community. The Henderson's major contribution was keeping Sheridan Elementary School open by funding the renovation of its building and facilities. Lenneal became an officer of the Holy Names Society of St. Michael's and St. Stephen's Churches in San Francisco. They were active in the Senior Network and the Ocean View Merced Heights Ingleside Neighbors in Action. Key awards often meant modest joy. When they received the Daniel Koshland Award for community betterment from the San Francisco Foundation, they were elated. Marcella started the Happy Hearts Club as a vehicle for senior citizens, and the Ingleside Presbyterian Church awarded her the 1999 Mother's Day Award for a lifetime of unconditional love and support and the spirit she had given their seven children.

Q & A: THE CURRY INTERVIEW

Lenneal and Marcella Henderson lived in a segregated society, yet they managed to maintain their own sense of faith, function, and freedom in their lives. They were not satisfied with finding few opportunities for success in New Orleans, where their first son, Lenneal Jr., and three more kids were born, so they moved to San Francisco. Lenneal worked as a Pullman porter and a cook, but once in San Francisco, he went back to school to study electronics and Marcella went to the Galileo Adult School to become a licensed vocational nurse (LVN).

Lenneal died in February 2004, and Marcella celebrated her eighty-seventh birthday in August 2011. Following is an edited transcript from an interview with their adult children , conducted in November, 2011.

Q: What was your dad's worst habit?

A: Lenneal Jr.: One habit Dad had turned him into a top electronics student. He read the intricate manuals and schematics out loud. It helped his memory. One side effect was he always talked to himself. When I turned nineteen years old, I decided to inquire about this habit to make sure he was doing all right health wise. He looks at me with piercing green eyes, explaining that, before each day ends, he was going to talk to at least one intelligent person. He decided it might as well be him.

Linda: Dad's worst habit as our father was whenever one of us had done something he felt was bad, the offender received a lecture that lasted for hours. I often would pray to myself, thinking it would be better to get this stuff over with a fast whipping. What a choice!

Q: What was his best advice?

A: Lenneal Jr:. He always taught me to pray and pursue a rich spiritual life. Taking me to men's retreats and, soon after, married couples' retreats, he set the tone by living that way himself. When I talked to him about dating young ladies, he told me to "just remember, when you're out there with a fine young lady, things can get hot and heavy. Puppy love leads to a dog's life." He [pointed out that he] now owns a kennel.

Linda: Dad's best advice was not in words but actions. He taught us:

- Family first! Stay together.
- Always see about your family members in times of need.
- Get an education.
- Take care of your possessions and your personal hygiene.
- Keep your house, clothes, and body clean and well groomed.

Q: What special memories or story would you like to tell of your parents?

A: Lenneal Jr.: The train ride from New Orleans to Oakland [was] so exciting! I am six years old. No matter that we are in the colored section of the train up to Arizona. I look out the window and see a world I did not know, snuggle up at night in the sleeper cars, and delight in the sound of the train whistle wailing in the middle of the night. The westbound train arrives in the Oakland rail yards. We board the ferry to San Francisco. I see the bridge painted red, the bright blue sky above us, sun shining all around, and the clear, rippling, blue water below us—another moment of wonderment.

Linda: Every moment with our parents was special. Momma told me [the following]:

- Always follow your dreams.
- Bury your hatchets when a family member is down or in need.
- Go to the aid of your brothers/sisters when they need you.
- Always 'be your own woman', honey, and 'don't let any man run over you'!

According to Eleanor Roosevelt, yesterday is history, tomorrow is a mystery, and today is a gift. That's why it is called the present. This exactly describes Mom."

Five Things to Know about The Henderson Parents.

The Henderson parents (1) held important jobs, (2) bought their house in 1959 in San Francisco but always loved to travel, (3) were habitual learners, (4) differed in that Marcella likes to watch television, while Lenneal loved to sleep in the afternoon, and (5) both loved playing Bingo.

Most of all, Lenneal and Marcella chose to pray daily and believe in God. How else could they have chosen to follow the straight and narrow road, plus be such good neighbors? Who is your good neighbor?

Why Did I Become a Maid?
Note: The names in the following stories have been changed.

"Eleanor, could you fill in as a housekeeper?" Maxine is "colored" and coordinates a maid service out of Hunter's Point, where she also lives. She is good at handling the white clients and the housekeepers she recommends.

"You get paid ten dollars plus bus fare. I have a request for Saturday from nine to five."

"Where do they live?" I ask. "How many people live there? When do I start?" Marcella will be glad for me when I tell her, I found a job.

"The woman lives on Sacramento Avenue with her little girl," Maxine continues. "You will be paid cash. She'll tell you what your duties will be. Can you begin next Saturday?"

"I'll be ready." I think of Mother's being a maid. If it is honest work and the only job you can get, take it. I decide that I'll be the best maid ever.

"Hello, Eleanor," the woman greeted me at the door. "I'm Mrs. Jordan. The main service shall be to Judy, my three-year-old daughter. She's too young for school. Normally on Saturdays, I have to rest in the afternoon. My extremely high-pressure job exhausts me. This is the only time I can relax." She seems sincere and pleasant.

"Where is Judy now?" I ask.

"She is with my mom. They should be back around noon. Do you have any questions?"

I look around the various rooms of the household. It seems almost too easy.

Judy has a desk and two small chairs off from the kitchen, so I am able to keep an eye on her while I am working. She arrives home in the early afternoon. She is a delightful child, I think, as I notice her inquisitive glance.

She has reddish hair, cut short, and big brown eyes and dimples when she smiles.

"Judy, come meet Eleanor," Mrs. Jordan says. "She is going see us every Saturday."

"Does she know Grandma?" Judy asks. She turns to an elegant, stylish woman who has been calmly observing us without comment.

"Sorry, Mom," Mrs. Jordan says as she turns to bring her mom into the conversation. She introduces both Judy and her mom to me. I start the next week.

A few months into the job, I arrive at nine in the morning to find that Judy is hollering at her mother. "You don't like me!" she yells. "You always stay in that room with the door closed. I'm going to tell Grandma! I hate you!"

Mrs. Jordan does not utter a word. Judy, who is crying, moves to her little chair and plunges herself into it, still upset. Mrs. Jordan shifts her eyes to me.

"Hello." She sounds pitiful. She mumbles, "I have a severe headache. I must rest early today. I'm glad you are here." She staggers to her bedroom, almost stumbling before she gets there. Judy watches with disdain. I realize that Mrs. Jordan is drinking too much alcohol and that this is probably why she is alone so much. I begin to clean the house.

"Eleanor, can we go out early today?" Judy asks just before she blows her nose. "Mama makes me sick."

"Judy, I have something very important to tell you." I feel sorry for the child, yet I cannot stand the way she talks to her mother. "We are not going anyplace until you apologize to your mother. I am surprised to hear such words coming from you."

"Oh, Eleanor, you don't know how she acts," Judy replies, looking perplexed. "She is mean when nobody else is with us. Grandma thinks I am too sassy with Mama. I will not apologize."

"We will not go walking or anywhere else until you do." I return to cleaning the house. Judy refuses to eat lunch, and Mrs. Jordan stays in her bedroom. The day passes. My work is finished, but Judy is still upset. She gets up out of her chair, walks over, and touches me on my right shoulder.

"When can I tell Mama?" she asks, looking miserable.

"Right now, Judy, since you're ready," I say. "Do you know what you want to say? Do you think we should knock on the door now or later?"

"Let's do it now, while you are here." Judy has the faint trace of a smile. "Do you think Mama is mad at me?"

"Time to go and see how she feels," I reply. "I hope her headache is gone." Just as we approach the closed bedroom door, it opens. Mrs. Jordan stands there, rubbing her eyes.

"Mama, I love you!" Judy says as she runs to her, grabs her, and hugs her. "I am so sorry. I'll never say anything like that to you ever again. Please forgive me." Mrs. Jordan and Judy hug each other, both feeling better. I am ready to leave since order has been restored. However, I was totally unprepared for the next devastating experience.

Two months pass, and I receive a rare call from Mrs. Jordan.

"Hello, Eleanor. I wanted to let you know, my husband works in England. He'll be in town when you come to work Saturday. I thought you should be aware that he might be here at the house. If he seems a bit strange, just ignore him."

"Thanks for calling," I say, concerned regarding what was not said. When I arrive on Saturday, everything is too quiet. Judy is not near her small table. I decide to clean up her space first, bending down to clear the table. Suddenly, I feel somebody's fists desperately beating on my back.

I turn to defend myself and grab the swinging arms in a split second. It's Judy, still swinging, crying, and screaming. I hold her at arm's length, looking around for her mother.

"What is the matter, Judy?" I ask. "This is Eleanor." I'm trying to get her under control.

"Let me go!" she cries. "You are going to kill me so you can eat me up." Her fears are blurted out through her screaming and crying. "You hate me! I can't be around you at all. You are not real. You are a scary nigger." I hold her but keep her a bit away from me too.

"Judy, I am your mother's housekeeper," I say. "You know my name. I am not what someone else told you. I will never hurt you." I am getting angry at the situation, wondering who is putting these ideas in her head. Then, a light bulb flashes in my mind—her daddy is in town.

"Let's go wash your face, Judy," I say. "Everything will be all right!"

"No, it won't." Judy has stopped crying, but she is still upset. "My daddy said I can't go anywhere else with you alone ever again. He said he knows what's best for me." She starts crying again.

Mrs. Jordan hears the commotion but does not react to what Judy's saying. We stare at each other.

"Has Judy had breakfast yet?" I ask. Mrs. Jordan shakes her head.

I prepare Judy's breakfast and coax her to eat. She has stopped crying, and I get her to sit at her table and start to play with her toys. She is listless. Mrs. Jordan and I move to the dining room, where we can still watch Judy.

"Please have a seat, Eleanor," she says, speaking low.

"Her dad was over all day yesterday. They were having a wonderful time together. They seemed happy, making plans to do so much since he's in town for only another week. Then he became annoyed with Judy when she told him she could not go with him on Saturday, because you always took her places. He went into a rage, glaring at both of us, demanding to know who this person, taking his child to some strange places. I did not know what to say. Once Judy answered his questions, he told her the things she said to you today." Now Mrs. Jordan starts to cry.

"Why did you allow your child to be subjected to his insanity?" I ask. I am anguished, annoyed, and astonished. "Why didn't you stop him?"

"He often would go into a slight rage when Judy was a baby. He has not seen her in two years. He didn't believe I had hired you. He told me not to trust any niggers and to get rid of you."

"I am not a nigger," I say. "The word is used to destroy people." I am vehement.

"I know that, Eleanor, but he even threatened to take Judy away from me. He kept raging at me after he scared Judy out of her wits."

"Why didn't you stop him?" I ask again. No answer. "I hope you know what this means," I say, thinking of Judy. "I will no longer work for you."

"Oh, no!" she cries. "He'll be leaving next week. Please don't quit. What will we do?"

"Call your mom. She'll help you with Judy." Now Mrs. Jordan is crying harder.

I go over to Judy and hug her close. Then I hold both her hands at a little distance.

"Judy, remember the good times we had," I tell her. "Remember how smart you are. Always remember to be good to your mom, no matter what happens. This is my last day."

Judy grabs me around my waist, holding me tight, and says quietly, "Bye, Eleanor."

Another Maid Job Is Ready

I tell Maxine the sad news and begin seeking another job. This time I ask, "Will any children be in the house?"

Maxine calls me back the following week. "The new assignment is for an older widow who still works part-time at a news office but has no children. The distance is a little farther and up a hill. You will have to drive a car or take a train. It is on Saturdays too."

Maxine had everything ready, and I began the following Saturday. Mrs. Sarah Benton, eighty-two years old, is alert, well bred, inquisitive, and an intensive listener. She is thrilled for me to be with her. She encourages me to go to college, because she loves the sound of my voice. She thinks I should study journalism and maybe be on the radio, because I have a calming effect on her. I laugh, and I say, "Thanks for your opinion, but for now, I'm educating our six children." I remain with her for more than a year. In the early spring, she decides we should talk before I start working.

"I have a niece who lives in New York," she says. "My younger brother wants me to bring her here for the summer. She and her mother are not getting along. I thought I should check with you before I answer him. What do you think?"

"This is your house and your family," I reply. "My work does not cover family issues. How old is your niece?"

"Oh, she'll be twenty-six years old on her next birthday." Mrs. Benton laughs. "After your large family, I understand you not wanting any small kids or teenagers on your job."

Melody, the niece, enters a tranquil world at Mrs. Benton's home. My first reaction when seeing Melody is to decide that she is gross. She is five feet tall and has thick, wheat-colored hair, sunburned skin, and thin lips in a straight line, without a hint of a smile. She weighs 240 pounds.

"Hello," she says. "You're the famous Eleanor my aunt Sarah keeps bragging about to my father." Melody talks fast, in a clip-chopped tone. "Let's have lunch on your break so we can get to know each other."

"Sorry, Melody," I reply. "We are not allowed to eat with our employers. Thanks for asking me."

"What? Do you always do as you are told?" she asks. "You must lead a dull, dull, dull life. Good grief."

Each week, Melody tempts me to go somewhere with her—to have lunch, to go see a movie, or go for a ride in Mrs. Benton's car.

"Melody, I am not here to befriend you," I tell her. "I am here to clean the house. The two of us cannot socialize."

"Eleanor, you are sickening, never having any fun. What's wrong with you? Oh, you must wait until my aunt orders you to do it. I'll go tell her right now that you refuse to respect me."

She wobbles out of the kitchen, looking for Mrs. Benton.

I am thinking. Something is wrong with this woman. She does not seem to understand a simple yes or no. I keep working until the day ends. Mrs. Benton calls my house on Monday.

"Eleanor, I'm leaving on a ten-day vacation in the morning. Do you think Melody can be with you until I return?" she asks.

"I am only there on Saturday," I answer. "She is grown. Why are you reluctant to leave her? Is anything wrong I need to know about?"

"Not really," she replies. "I'll leave an extra door key and your salary with Mrs. Pamela across the street. I'll be back in two weeks."

On Saturday, I go through the back patio door toward the house. I open the gate and stop dead in my tracks as

I look around the small yard. It is in shambles—broken glasses, feathers scattered all over, eggshells splattered across the windows, a mattress ripped to pieces and laying sideways. I freeze, thinking, Melody has been hurt. She might be dead. I cannot go in there. What could have happened? I shut the gate fast and rush across the street to Mrs. Pamela's house. She opens the door before I can knock.

"Something terrible has happened," I say. "I think somebody broke into Mrs. Benton's house. Did you hear anything during the night?" I pause and then say, "Melody could be hurt or dead."

"Sit down, Eleanor," Mrs. Pamela says, too quietly. "I think Melody had a few friends over at two a.m. this morning. It was terribly loud, but we were afraid to call the police. That might upset Mrs. Benton. They left at six thirty this morning. What are you going to do?"

"Have you seen the patio?" I ask. Mrs. Pamela shakes her head. "I'll go and check out the house," I say.

I am still apprehensive. I open the front door and see that the living room is torn up worse than the patio. It looks like a tornado had struck without destroying the outer frame of the house. I am reluctant to move any farther. I can see a section of the kitchen, and the chaos there is just as bad. I am not going to clean this house today.

The phone hanging on the kitchen wall rings, grabbing my attention.

"Hello," I say. "Who's speaking?"

"Eleanor, hi. I'm so glad you came today," Melody says. "We had a little party, and it got a bit rough. I am on my way home, be there in ten minutes, so we can clean things up. It shouldn't take us…" Fast-talking Melody will not stop, so I interrupt.

"Melody, stop and listen to me. We are not going to clean up the house. You made this mess. You clean it up. I'm leaving as soon as we hang up."

"Wait a minute," she says. "You are the maid. That's your job. Don't you dare leave. Do you understand my order?"

"Good-bye, Melody!" I hang up the phone, lock the door, and leave. I tell Mrs. Pamela my plans, and she hands me my salary, rather sad. "Mrs. Benton would want you to have this. Are you coming in next week when she returns?"

"I'll call first," I reply. "Thanks for your help."

The following Saturday, Mrs. Benton is up early when I get to the house.

"Oh, Eleanor, after the situation with my niece, are you going to quit?" she asks nervously.

"Why would I quit?" I ask. "You didn't do anything." I'm thinking about how much we need the ten dollars and bus fare she pays me every week. "Are you trying to fire me?" I am nervous, too.

"Oh, no," she says. "I'm so glad you will stay. You're one of the best maids I've ever had. I can get you more work with a few of my friends. Today at your break, let's have lunch together."

I am relieved but must have looked shocked and surprised about lunch.

"I know this is not the way it's supposed to be, but, after all, it is my house, so we'll eat together." She continues, "Melody has gone back to New York. She was having a rough time. My car was also beyond repair. What do you think will happen to her?" Mrs. Benton is calm yet uncertain.

"I have no idea," I say, pushing my food around on my plate. "You did your part." I am curious about her family.

"My brother paid for all the damages plus bought me another car," she says. "You're right. This is over."

Mrs. Benton calls me the following Monday.

"Eleanor, I wanted to talk to you before Saturday. My brother has to come to San Francisco on a business trip. He wants to know if you could come to my house for dinner Friday evening. Would your husband mind?" She keeps talking. "In fact, you can spend the night and be here for Saturday. Or a better plan might be coming for dinner and take Saturday off—with pay, of course."

"Wait a minute," I say, hesitant. "This is too fast for me."

"I know I sound too eager," she says. "But this would mean so much to us."

I agree to come Friday evening and take Saturday as a rest day.

Friday is warm, and there's a slight breeze in the late evening—perfect weather. When I get to Mrs. Benton's house, her brother is ready to meet me. I am surprised at my first impression of him. He could pass for Clarke Gable: tall, handsome, relaxed, and well mannered. I think. This could not be Melody's father. How did she get so heavy? Mrs. Benton interrupts my thoughts.

"Eleanor, we're pleased to have you here. This is Mr. Cedric Wellington, my brother." She turns toward him and says, "Cedric, this is Eleanor." We both smile and shake hands.

"You may call me Cedric if you like, since we both respect my sister, Sarah," Mr. Wellington, a perfect gentleman, says. "Will that work for you, too?" he asks, turning toward Mrs. Benton. She agrees. We have an incredible time. Mrs. Benton serves orange sherbet for dessert. Then, Mr. Wellington, in a level tone, asks, "Eleanor, can you tell me what you remember about the situation with you and Melody?" I become quiet, and he continues, "I have heard her version. I would appreciate your comments. There's something I must do, but I want to be factual." I am still quiet, saying nothing.

"Let me be straight," he offers. "There will not be any trouble for you. I respect Sarah's opinion of your character. There are always two sides to a story. I need your side. Let me ask a question. How did you say no to Melody?" Reassured, I share the entire episode.

"I knew she was lying again," he says, obviously open minded. "I know what I must do now. Thanks for helping me rethink Melody's life." I fall quiet again, uncertain what that means. Earl picks me up at nine o'clock that evening.

The following week, I am anxious to get to work. Mrs. Benton is so glad to see me that she hugs me the minute I get in the house.

"Eleanor, Cedric was thrilled with everything that transpired last week. The family has been upset with her actions since she was a little girl. They have spent countless dollars bailing her out of frantic situations. His wife told him Melody was not acting normal years ago. You are the first person to say no to her, which got Cedric's attention. He immediately checked her into a mental hospital, hoping it will save her life."

We are both speechless and full of joy. I continue to be Mrs. Benton's housekeeper until about one year later, when she dies of natural causes.

My last job as a maid is my best one. Mrs. Benton introduces me to Mrs. Angelia Manning, who is married and has one teenage daughter. After just six weeks with her family, she decides that I should no longer work for her.

"Eleanor, I thought of you all week long," she says. "Why are you working as a maid?"

"I'm helping my husband feed our family," I reply.

"I have another idea for you. You are intelligent and articulate with a wonderful attitude. You should find a job to match you for the person you are."

"It is not that easy," I say, feeling grateful yet desperate. "Few people will hire colored people. We were seldom allowed on the other side of town in Missouri, where I came from. Most of the few jobs did not pay us as much as I'm getting now. Thanks for the kind remarks, but what can I do?"

"You can volunteer for a short time," she says. "This will get people to know you. I have a friend that will be just right for you. I'll call her and see what happens. Are you ready?"

"You sure know how to make people laugh!" I say with a smile and go back to finishing for the day. The next month, my whole world changes as I shift into the world of volunteering. Four years afterward, better jobs come to me.

President John F. Kennedy

The year is 1963, and I am preparing a speech for my sixteen-year-old daughter's history class. I think of the inspiring words that our newest president of the United States recently said, knowing such a message would be perfect for the students: "Ask not what your country can do for you, but what you can do for your country."

Three weeks later, I check the noontime television news and hear, "Our thirty-fifth president, John F. Kennedy, has been shot in a motorcade in Dealey Plaza, in Dallas, Texas." I am terrified and numb. I close my eyes, thinking, He's too young and full of life. Who could have done this and why? Then another blast of news comes: "The president is dead." I'm too shocked to move. Tears roll down my face.

Curry Spice: "Everything from local happenings to national events, can cause one to be glad, mad, or sad. The president's death made me too sad.

CHAPTER SEVEN
1964–1969
Transformational Timing in the Suburbs

New House, New Hope

We buy a new house that has two bedrooms, one bath, and a large room on the second floor. Our new address is 33 North Fremont Street, in the city of San Mateo. We soon realize this house is too small, yet has a large lot. My husband decides to renovate it, transforming it into a duplex. He starts with a two-bedroom apartment in the back of our lot and then adds a large room over the garage so our sons could sleep up there. Next he will finish work on the front house. The main house will have three bedrooms and two bathrooms, and a long back porch. But, it's not long before a major problem enters the plans: he needs to buy the blueprints, which cost nearly one thousand dollars. However, since I majored in industrial arts, I know about drawing buildings. "I can do the blueprints," I say. He is thrilled that I have such a skill. He tells me his innermost thoughts, and I complete the task. The building department approves the floor plans. We are ready to go. He proceeds to build the largest duplex in the city's history. We call it the house love built.

New Job

"Go to the top person when you want an important decision made." Mother's rule rings in my head. I make an appointment to meet with Mr. Hal DePue, superintendent of the San Mateo Elementary School District, when I decide to seek employment in the district. The year is 1966.

"I am new in town," I tell him. "Do you have any job openings? I need a job, but I can't take any more tests." I am confident yet nervous.

"Exactly what type of job, and why can't you take any tests?" he asks.

"I've held many positions as a volunteer and a community leader," I explain. "When searching for a paying job, I keep hearing, 'You are not qualified,' 'You're too young', 'too old,' or 'had too many children.' No more tests for me."

"How many kids do you have?"

"Eight kids—three daughters and five sons," I reply. "I am good with children. None of our kids have ever been in jail. That should count for some qualification."

"Have a seat in my outer office," he says. "I have a few calls to make."

Once Mr. DePue is on the telephone, I'm thinking, I have a lot of nerve. I may never get this job, whatever it may be.

"I have good news for you," he says after calling me in from the outer office. "We have an opening to get you started. It is a teacher's aide position. You can see if you like it and then work your way up from there." I was speechless but managed a smile.

"Can you start next Monday?" he asks. Mr. DePue is smiling. "One more thing, no tests." We both laugh.

I am a brand new teacher's aide. I am assigned to an all-white suburban school, where the principal greets me to give me my assignments. I am to work with two kindergarten teachers who both have too many children in their classes.

"If you have any trouble," he says and then hesitates as if searching for the right words, "just come tell me. Check out the teachers' lounge. You're free to go there. See you later."

"Thanks," I say. "I'm ready." I wonder. What is he trying to tell me? First, I head to the teachers' lounge so I'll know where it is.

"Hello," a woman with wheat-colored hair and bangs says with a smile. "Are you the new janitor assistant?" She is sitting at a table with stacks of papers.

"No, I'm the new teacher's aide," I reply.

"Oh, my goodness," she says. She jumps up, causing the papers to fly off the table.

"Here let me help you," I say as I reach to pick them up.

"Don't touch my papers," she says in a whisper full of fear.

I stand there, not moving.

Once she collects her papers, she rushes out of the lounge.

Maybe this is why the principal seemed hesitant. I walk quickly to my first class.

A Child Asks, "What Is She?"
"Hello, Mrs. Curry." A five year-old girl says, few days later." I told mama about you looking like my teacher and talking like her, except you are very dark. I ask her, what are you?

"Come stand by me," she continues. "I'll help you say the Pledge of Allegiance so you learn about our country."

Here I am, an African American woman, born in America, with a family of eight kids and deeply concerned about education right where we live. How can I make a contribution to the district and the kids when they are awestruck and wondering 'what is she"?

Some days, I mix paint, read a story to the kids, or help with a puppet show. My role depends on the needs of the two teachers. During the lunch hour, I organize games and supervise the playing of older students. Probably my most valuable function is giving what I call "sneak attention." So many kids need one-on-one time, but the teachers have planned teaching lessons. Their schedules do not allow time for the restless, shy, or lonely youngsters who need an extra amount of encouragement or individual attention. I fill in such gaps with a special comment, a kind word, a smile, or gentle assistance.

The small children are at first polite and curious, just observing me, too polite, I think later. Whenever I catch their eyes, they look away. But once they're comfortable, they ask questions without even thinking. Rarely are the questions insulting or malicious; they're mostly hesitant, spontaneous, and honestly in search of answers. I am learning, too, about how I can best use my skills for each teacher and the individual children. I am appreciative of the children who want to know more about me.

"Were you ever a baby?" a five-year-old girl asks.

"Yes," I reply with a nod.

"Were you ever a little girl?"

I nod again.

"Boy am I glad." She looks relieved and runs away, happy.

Many others find it hard to believe that my hands are not dirty. I am really brown all over. Most decide that I must be from Africa.

Whenever it is warm enough to eat outside, I monitor the students from the fourth grade too.

"Hello, Aunt Jemima," one nine-year-old boy wisecracks.

"How are you today, Bob Hope?" I respond as I throw the big ball to him.

"My name is not Bob Hope!" he retorts angrily.

"My name is not Aunt Jemima," I reply. The next week, he wants to know my name. I make him the manager of putting the big ball in the locker, and we become good friends.

"Mrs. Curry, Mrs. Curry," says Sandy, a five-year-old, running faster than normal and waving her arms with excitement. She's running so fast that I spread both arms wide to catch her and prevent a fall.

"Hello, Sandy. What is the matter?" I catch her, holding her close. Her heart is pumping. "Calm down," I say. "What is it?"

"I thought you were all alone in our world," she begins. She smiles and rushes on. "I saw another woman just like you on TV last night. I won't worry about you anymore."

"I still haven't figured what you are, but you're nice," one five-year-old boy tells me eight

months later, very relaxed.

Then, during lunchtime on another day, a ten-year-old boy says, "Hey, Mrs. Curry, you're pretty keen. But there's one thing wrong with you." I hold my breath. "You're too full of rules," he finishes.

One year later, I feel accepted as part of the school structure when an extremely shy six-year-boy says at recess, "Mrs. Curry, you're just like an old teacher." That's a compliment.

More than ever before in my life, I'm convinced we have much to learn from one another. Working at the school is a bittersweet, shattering introduction to an experience that turned out to be rewarding and revealing. I hope it was also constructive for the children who initially thought I was someone from a foreign country or even a museum.

Human Relations Specialist

Twelve years after the 1954 Brown v. Board of Education court ruling that all public schools across the country are to become integrated, San Mateo begins implementing its plan.

Once I complete the teacher aide assignment in 1967, I am hired to be a Human Relations Specialist with the San Mateo elementary school District. When I read the job description, I know this is not going to be an ordinary job. The priority mission is described this way: "to service all of the students in the twenty-three public schools with the desegregation concept."

It is 1968. I am sitting at my desk at work, about to complete the script for a skit for the gifted class on nonviolence as a profound diversity tool. The next afternoon at home, I hear over my radio the latest news flash: "Dr. Martin Luther King Jr. has just been shot standing on a balcony outside his room at the Lorraine Hotel in Tennessee. He was struck by a sniper's bullet." Tears stream from my eyes. I am still crying an hour later when the telephone rings. "Is this Mrs. Curry?" a new friend asks. "Are you doing all right? Are you crying?"

"Yes, please excuse me," I reply. "Someone just shot Dr. King. I'll be fine."

"Oh, that's why I'm calling. What can we do?" She is crying too.

"Since he was a man of peace, pray and light a candle tonight," I tell her. Then I am quiet.

Calls about Dr. King's death came over the entire week at our home. We told all who called to light a candle.

Gifted Class Awakening

"Eleanor, I heard of the diversity classes you offer students at my grade level," the principal at the middle school, who is very supportive of the Human Relations Program, says. "Have you spent time with any gifted classes yet?"

"Yes," I say, "but I have not been to your school."

"All these seventh-grade students go from high school straight to college. I want them to have an opportunity to meet you."

Three days later, on a Friday morning, I face twenty gifted students, boys and girls. They are called the brightest and the best.

"Good morning," I begin. "My name is on the blackboard if you have any questions as we proceed."

"Mrs. Curry," one student interjects. "I have a few questions before we get started. I heard you are going to explain new material covering diversity and getting along with people different from one's self." He's smooth, and he starts talking faster. "When I heard the subject, I did some research. I believe you're wasting your time with us. You need to go talk to your own people and teach them how to read so they can stop stealing and landing in jail." He twirls a pencil around as he stares at me. The total silence makes the air-conditioner suddenly loud in the room.

"How did you come to such exact conclusions?" I ask calmly.

"Well, they must all be pretty stupid," he replies. "I knew that before the research."

"Have you ever met any of these people you describe as my own people?" I ask.

"I have been in gifted classes since I was five years old. Not a single colored person has ever been in my classes, so they must all be dumb."

At that, a few other students find their voices. "Are you kidding? Knock it off," one says. Another student offers, "I play basketball with two of them. They are the best. They are not stupid."

Others chime in: "Watch out, Mr. Know-it all. Let the teacher show us a different way." "Yeah, be quiet. You don't know that much. You get on my last nerve."

I clap my hands to restore order. I decide to change my normal approach. I read "Ten Facts of Diversity" to fill the remaining time.

Before class is over, I say, "I will bring a group of colored gifted students in next week. Be prepared for a few debates in groups of five. You will not be in groups with each other. You will be in groups with the guests I'll invite." The bell rings, and class is dismissed.

I set up my next visit with the principal for Tuesday morning, requesting two hours instead of forty-five minutes. 'Values Clarification' is a game book developed especially for sixth graders to twelfth graders and designed to give students a healthy communication tool for conversing within the group setting.

When Tuesday comes, I am prepared. "Good morning, everyone," I begin. "I'm going to put you into groups of five. Once in the assigned team, please write your first name on a name tag and introduce yourself. When everyone is finished, raise your hand. We'll be ready to start the game."

The game is set up around the scenario that the world is coming to an end. Ten people are on an island, destined to start another world. The problem is that only six people can be saved, and the players' task is to determine which six will live and explain why they are chosen. The people are a cafeteria cook, a doctor, a firefighter, a police officer, a rabbi, a television newscaster, a scientist, a soldier, a teacher, and an unmarried, pregnant sixteen-year-old.

There are five groups, and each has a chosen leader. After the students discuss for twenty minutes, I call for order. "Time is up. Take a break. Be ready for an open discussion." One student immediately starts negotiating for the one person he feels must be saved as the class moves around right outside the classroom.

The students return to the classroom gets in their regular seats. Beaming and buzzing with bated breaths, I say to them. "Get ready, get set, and go."

The five group leaders march to the front, three colored and two white students. The final lists of choices are close. All the groups eliminated the rabbi "because he's going to heaven no matter what happens." They also all saved the pregnant teenager "because we know she can help start a new world." The cafeteria cook was saved, and they justified this choice, saying, "Because the others have to eat, and she can feed them."

"Why were you trying to save the cook even during the break?' I ask one of the colored students.

"Oh, that's because my mother does that kind of work, and she's good." Everybody laughs.

The gifted Jewish student turns to speak to the colored students. "You guys are smart. How come you've never been in any gifted classes?"

"Are you kidding?" the ten students reply at once. One continues, "The teachers put too many bad labels on us to keep us out."

The students shake hands, smiling and full of glee. This classroom experiment is successful, getting everyone an "E" for excellent.

Curry Spice: Eyes see, ears listen, mouths talk. The best is just being there to walk with each other.

CHAPTER EIGHT
1970–1975
Local High School Racial Drama

I pick up the telephone at eight thirty one morning and find that one of my sons is having a conversation with a friend, who says, "Man, are you okay? We are ready to pay them back for hitting you with that chair. We'll do whatever you want us to do."

I hang up the phone, surprised at what I just heard. I rush to my husband in our bedroom.

"Something is wrong," I say. "Talk to Arnold right now." I call our son and tell him that his daddy needs to see him before he leaves for school.

"Hello, Arnold," my husband says. "What's going on with you?" He waits patiently.

"I was standing in the hall between classes. A white dude starts yelling at me, grabs a chair, and hits me in the head. The nurse checked me out. The principal suspended him, and that's it."

"Your mother thinks otherwise," my husband replies. "Until she checks this out, you are on home duty."

"But Daddy, I have to be at school so I won't miss my class work."

"Your mother will pick up whatever you need. That's it. You are grounded until we know both sides of the situation."

As the chairperson of the San Mateo Human Relations Commission, I have to be available to the high school district. The same day that I overheard my son's conversation, a mass meeting is held at the Martin Luther King Community Center in San Mateo. The parents and other community leaders arrive with their teenage students, over 250 strong. Eighty percent of the attendees are African Americans. Most of the officials are ten percent white. The capacity is three hundred.

The high school students speak first, attempting to explain their anger, anxiety, and sense of a dilemma about the incident involving my son. Next, a young adult, a cinnamon-colored, heavyset, black man, appears at the microphone. "I want to let you know, there'll be no more running over our people if we hear of it. Anyone, anywhere, or anymore shall not ever torment our brothers. We want everyone present to spread the word. We came to stop abuses of…" Another guy comes to the mike, thinner, interrupts, holding a note and pointing at various spots in the audience.

The speaker stares at the audience. He uses a booming voice.

"I know most of you here tonight are not students," he says. "When things happen to the students, they have to be straightening out by them. All of you over thirty years old, please leave now!"

I cannot believe my ears or my eyes. The adults start moving from the large room. The audience shrinks to half its original size as the people exit. I sit there, very quiet, sure something ugly is going to happen. I feel strapped into my seat.

The thinner man glances over the remaining crowd, whispering to the speaker.

I am sitting on the right side, in the back of the room and near the exit, wondering where these two people have come from. They do not live in San Mateo. I know most of the families by sight. This situation does not look good, more like trouble.

"Hey, you back there. I told everybody over thirty to leave now!" he shouts as he glares at me. I look behind me. I sit taller, returning my focus with a deep silence.

"How old are you, woman?" He's getting louder and pointing at me.

"I'm twenty-nine years old," I reply. Louder laughter stops him from responding. Student voices shout in unison, as if rehearsed, "That's Mrs. Curry. She's our friend. She's different. Let her stay."

The plan is laid out: Bring any weapon you can hide under your jacket to school tomorrow. If anybody dares to cross you, hit them with whatever you brought with you. If policemen are around, do not resist them. If you end up in jail, do a silent protest.

I have heard enough. I move from my seat toward the front, and then I ask for the mike.

"Here is one more item to add to that list," I said. "If you happen to go to jail, which I'm certain you will, do not call any parents to bail you out. We parents are doing everything in our power to help you get an education. We do not have any extra money to throw away. Don't call us. Good night." I walk straight to the door, get in my car, and drive the two blocks home.

Before I enter the high school the next morning, the school grounds are surrounded with police officers. The principal is waiting for me at the main entrance to the school.

"Hello, Mrs. Curry," the principal said. I am glad you came early. I need you to be the Mistress of Ceremony for today's assembly. There are going to be approximately twelve hundred students, teachers, and other community leaders present."

"Wait a minute." I'm speechless for a second. "What are you going to be doing in case I need you?"

"I'll be intermingling among the guests who plan to be present," he says. "I don't want the students to think I'm taking sides. I know you will remain neutral."

Unlike last night, the audience is over eighty percent White, three percent Oriental students and fifteen percent African Americans.

I do not feel prepared for this task with such a large gathering. I think of last night at the community center. I move to a dark section of the stage and close my eyes to ask God to guide me through this one. I hear someone approaching me and open my eyes to see a light-skinned colored police officer coming near me.

"Hello," he says. "Aren't you the new person on the Human Relations Commission for the City?"

"Yes, and this is my first big assignment," I reply.

"So you're another one of those do-gooders, right? You could be in way over your head on this one."

As if I need his negative vibe to get me in the best frame of mind, I merely stare at him. Silent, I wait for his next comment.

"Don't stress out. I have been ordered to remain on the stage with you," he says while smiling. "If things get rough, I'll be here as a backup, behind the curtain, of course."

The stage is set. The goal is to have the students air their concerns and restore peace on campus. The students are angry, full of blaming, and in a critical dilemma. They are ready to strike out at anyone near them. Whenever a student comes to the mike to speak, others shout out things like, "That's a lie," "You are stupid," "You are making that lie up," "You were nowhere near the stuff," and "Sit down, you phony."

"Wait a minute." I bang the gavel for order. "We need to get ourselves under control. Repeat this statement after me. When I count to three, I want all of you to repeat these words. Are you ready?"

"Yes," they said in thunderous unison.

"Every man thinks he's right in his mind, but God ponders our heart. 1, 2, 3!"

All twelve hundred voices shout back the verse.

"Now," I say, "we shall be fair to each other. Wait your turn. You can ask questions, but no more booing, shouting, or yelling."

Everyone is in serious conversation from nine thirty to noon. The police officer on the stage with me walks toward me.

"All the weapons have been collected from the white kids," he says. "You can close the assembly. One more thing: you are more than a do-gooder." He salutes and moves off the stage.

I close the assembly. I feel breathless and lightheaded. I shut my eyes.

'Thank you, God, for guiding me'. Imagine! No casualties. Peace is restored.

Curry Spice: When you know right from wrong, hold on, hold on, hold on for right.

CHAPTER NINE
1976–1981
REDISCOVERING FAMILY AND FRIENDS

"Life is no joke. But there sure is a lot of laughter along the way." This voice mail greeting is on Clifford's phone, my oldest brother, who lives in Chicago, Illinois. Clifford is a minister, an educational counselor, and a chaplain for area prisons, which he has been visiting for over twenty-five years. He thinks life is a joke. Ministers cannot think life is a joke because, well, they're ministers. They have to be serious. Or do they?

I recall two vital lessons I learned from being around Clifford. When he joined the U.S. Army to protect our country in World War II, he had to live with the white soldiers for the first time. Four of them spent much time together in a foxhole. They learned to live and breathe with one another.

"I'll never forget the day the enemy fired on our territory," he told me once. "I witnessed two of my buddies being killed right before my eyes. The other one was hurt very bad. I tried to shield the last one hit, when a piece of flying metal hit me in my right thigh. The rescue team found us, carried us to the hospital barracks, and saved our lives. I made a decision that day never to hate anyone ever in life, regardless of any social situation I would find myself in. Next thing I knew, I became a minister."

I did not know how deeply Clifford cares or how well he shows kindness and appears powerful until we experienced death together, when two family members died less than a year apart.

I think back to the time, when Lois Mae Carroll, our oldest sister, age seventy-six, was suffering from Alzheimer's and living in a nursing home in Chicago. She died in her sleep. I made plane reservations to be with Cliff and his wife, Cordetta, whom I had never met. We spent ten days together, and Cliff was full of joy because Cordetta and I liked each other and started becoming friends. They decided to vacation the following summer at our house in California.

Cordetta was a healthy size twelve and walked daily. She was energetic and ready for the trip. Before the summer ended, I called to check on their plans to come to our house.

"Hi, Cliff," I said. "When are you and Cordetta coming out here?" No response. "Cliff?" There's total silence. "Cliff, can you hear me?"

"Eleanor," Cliff says, sounding far, far away and breathing hollowly. "Oh Eleanor. Cordetta is no longer with me." I hold the phone, wondering what is going on.

"What are you talking about?" I match his shallow breathing. It could not be a divorce. It could not be death. She is too healthy.

"She told me six weeks ago," Cliff says, bewildered. I imagine the scene as he tells me the story.

"She has a pain that won't go away in her lower back. I took her to the hospital several times, but nothing was found to be out of the ordinary. She was in such severe pain that the staff called in a Chinese neurologist consultant. He went into an intense study. After the research, he told me to bring her in for another forty-eight hours to run a few more tests. The next day, he found the problem. There is a malignant tumor beneath the underlining of her liver. She has cancer. But it is too late to operate.

"I asked the doctor what I could do, and he told me, the best thing to do is pick her up in the morning. He was full of compassion, and told me, to keep her as comfortable as I can. They will watch her through the night.

Cliff continued. "I thanked him and then started searching for her favorite dress so I could get ready to bring her home the next day. But the phone rang at 6:22 a.m. It was the doctor, telling me, that he wanted to talk to me himself. He paused, before letting me know that Cordetta had quietly slipped away about an hour before.

Cliff and I become closer as we cry there on the phone together. Months later, he says to me, "Sometimes when those we love are taken away from us, God knows what we need, and often after a lost one, he sends something better."

Cliff meets Lillian, a beautiful retired schoolteacher with two daughters and one grandchild. They become engaged and then get married on Valentine's Day, 2003. They celebrate their eighth wedding anniversary on February 14, 2011.

Who Is Carmaleit Oakes?

I am now, in the eighties, working as the public affairs director at KSOL-Radio in San Mateo. I often represent the station at various community affairs and functions. One seldom knows when the past shall meet the present.

A request comes from the Bell-Haven Senior Center in East Palo Alto, a community apparently having a hard time educating elementary school children. More than seventy percent of them are performing below grade level. The mothers and grandparents feel hopeless, and my task is to inspire them and give them new courage to move ahead.

My key message is along these lines: "If a child has only one significant person during their early school life that believes in them, regardless of the child's status in life, they shall be productive. I want to tell you of a fourth-grade teacher I had. We still lived in the era of the Great Depression. I was one of those kids often going to school hungry and cold, depending on the weather. Our teacher made us wash our hands in cold water on extremely cold days, made us say the Pledge of Allegiance to the flag every morning, and made us sing 'God Bless America.' This was every day, before we did schoolwork assignments. Her name was Miss Delaney." The entire crowded room applauds.

Now is the time for questions and responses. Between questions, one elderly lady from the audience comes up the stairs and walks directly to me. I glance at her as she speaks.

"Would your name have been Eleanor Williams?" she asks.

"Miss Delaney!" I shout, too surprised to remain calm. "What are you doing in California?"

I grab her and lift her up, and then I remember the audience. "This is the teacher I was telling you I had in the fourth grade," I explain. Clapping hands and stomping feet are heard from every corner of the large room.

We both wait until the crowd leaves from the large room to spend a few moments together.

"What are you doing in California?" she asks immediately. "I'd like to know more of your plans, too. I am married. I have a daughter and a son. My married name is Carmaleit Oakes."

"I am married, too," I reply. Mrs. Oakes laughs when she hears of our large family. "What are you doing currently?" I ask. "Are you retired?" I am fascinated at having found her.

"I am a member of the East Palo Alto Citizens Committee on Incorporation, a group formed to promote the city's incorporation. I'm working on writing the incorporation papers for East Palo Alto. The area has become too large to stay unincorporated. Practically everything that happens here is under the control of the San Mateo County Board of Supervisors. Too many things seldom get done, or so much that's needed just does not ever materialize to benefit this place." She pauses.

"This has to be exciting for those of you doing it," I say. "How are things going as you work on this issue?" I am thinking of a possible radio program.

"We have a major problem," she offers, and then she hesitates. I encourage her to continue.

"Most of the people are afraid to vote, some are not sure how to vote, and some probably never have voted." She stops, looking concerned.

"Anyone opposed to the incorporation?"

"Are you kidding? My goodness, yes. That's a big part of the fear. They are afraid they'll lose their jobs or homes, and only God knows the other fears." I have heard enough.

"Give me a few names of the opposition," I tell her. "I will arrange a public affairs program to encourage people to vote. Due to FCC rules and regulations, we have to present both sides, remaining neutral." We set a date. Mrs. Oakes is pleased at the turn of events.

The entire area is saturated with news of the upcoming two-part series to air prior to the next election. I tagged the endings with three reasons to always be ready to vote: (1) we are somebody; (2) your vote is a private choice that only you know; and (3) the ballot is stronger than the bullet. I add that this is a top priority according to Benjamin Franklin. The final day arrives with both sides brimming with tension, hoping to score a victory.

On June 14, 1983, the San Mateo County Board of Supervisors declares that a measure to incorporate the community of East Palo Alto has passed by a margin of fifteen votes. Carmaleit Oakes is overjoyed.

On August 21, 1986, three years later, a lawsuit is filed with the Supreme Court of California. According to Justia US Law, the appellants seek to invalidate the municipal incorporation election on the grounds that there were irregularities in the handling of certain absentee ballots. The trial court found no violation of any mandatory provision of the Elections Code or tampering or fraud involving the ballots, and it affirmed the passage of the incorporation measure. The lawyers state, "We agree."

Carmaleit Oakes became known as a leader in the successful election to incorporate East Palo Alto. After teaching for forty-four years in the public school system in St. Louis, Missouri, I am thrilled that we met again, recalling the tremendous impact she had on my life. She instilled a positive self-image in all of her students. She believed that "equality starts with each of us and education is the door." In spite of living in the segregated area of the South, she always gave her best to others.

According to the Palo Alto Weekly, she became a community activist upon moving to East Palo Alto, participating in court hearings, numerous government meetings, and voter registration drives. Three key board member organizations she joined were the Community Development Institute, the Girls Club, and the East Palo Alto Senior Citizens Club.

Right before her eighty-ninth birthday, on April 10, 1995, Sister Oakes died at Stanford Hospital. Something she said has endured: "We worked hard to create a city. And we old-timers are going to stay here, develop it, and die peacefully, knowing each of us did our part."

Curry Spice: Family and friends stimulate our living, both in new encounters and in death. Keep giving.

CHAPTER TEN
1980–2000
COMMUNITY HARMONY

VALUES OF WOMEN

The Women's Council is full of dramatic encounters behind the scenes. It is composed of a dozen women who have decided to become an integral part of the San Mateo County government. We present our proposal to create a Women's council to focus on affairs critical to women to the county's Board of Supervisors. The Board vote 3–2 against it. We are full of despair, disgust, and dismay.

A few years later, in 1978, a young woman, the legal aide to Congressman Leo Ryan, narrowly escapes death in the Guyana tragedy. She returns home, thankful that she was not killed. She decides to run for an empty seat on the County Board of Supervisors. Her name is Jackie Speier, and we become a support team for her.

"If I win, what do you think women want?" she asks, and then she listens intently.

"I'd like for the government to do something on behalf of women and children." We say. "We are fed up with not getting our issues on the agenda. We often wonder if we should even deal with the government."

"You deal with the government every day when you travel on the roads or call a police officer, so you might as well stay with it," she responds with a laugh. "Let's get back to business."

Jackie Speier wins her seat in 1980, and she puts our proposal up for another vote. This time, the vote is 5–0 in our favor, and we are overjoyed. We are ready for business now.

The next woman to run for public office is Anna Eshoo. We have lunch together, shortly after, she wins the election. Never underestimate the power of a one-on-one luncheon. Incredible things start to happen. Supervisor Eshoo believes we must focus on creating something that highlights the needs of the less fortunate as well as recognizes women's talents and their contributions. The Women's Hall of Fame becomes the next most significant and instant success in San Mateo County.

The original Women's Council commissioners bring our hearts' concerns forth to explore the issues of life, which lead to work plans designed to address the needs of women in our county:

1. Feminization of poverty (many told us poverty did not exist in this county)
2. Child care for working moms
3. Domestic violence (we held public workshops)
4. Caregivers (caretakers become overwhelmed taking care of the sick)
5. Reproductive choice (still a major concern)
6. Child support and child custody
7. Education in math and science for young girls
8. Women and AIDS (how it affects their health)
9. The changing family structure (including public hearings from the state)

10. Teenage mothers (what is necessary to complete their education)

The community harmony is magnificent due to Janet Frakes, the expert staff leader of the San Mateo County Government Center. Janet is an excellent communicator and keeps us on target. These years are a highlight of my life. Many of the other women involved are still friends of mine as we move on to other positive endeavors.

THE UNITED WAY
The United Way is one of the top ten foundations in the United States in terms of assets, according to Forbes Magazine. Thomas (Tom) Ruppanner, president of United Way of the Bay Area, is an authentic advocate of equality for all citizens. Tom shares a magnitude of assistance that never comes to light unless the recipients tell their stories. I am a member of the Board of United Way, representing the County of San Mateo, and I soon realize the power of the genuine, humble, and kind man who leads the organization. He gains acclaim for being a multicultural employer when it is not popular in corporate America.

He oversees more than eight hundred volunteers, plus the integrated staff and consultants, to lead the Bay Area, which covers nine counties in California. The United Way's major mission as a community fund- raising foundation is to donate both restricted and unrestricted funds to thousands of nonprofit programs.

Once I am given the rules and regulations of the board, I make every effort to do my best. For the first few months, I am full of questions at the monthly lunchtime meetings.

"Eleanor," President Ruppanner says, "please come to my office if you are not in a hurry. I'd like to explain a few things to you." He appears relaxed. "It won't take too long." I follow him to his office.

"Good to have you as a new board member," he begins. "Any questions on your mind you'd like to discuss?"

"I asked them in the meeting. I can't think of one thing now."

"That's amazing. I just wanted to talk with you about all those questions. When you came on the board, what did your mentor instruct you to do?" He waits and smiles.

"He told me to pay attention, ask questions, and just tell the truth," I reply.

"Well you certainly are doing that!" Tom says as he laughs out loud. "Most questions are asked before the public meeting. There is not enough time in the meetings to cover too many questions. We have someone present the issue, make a motion, call for a second. The vote is ayes or nays, and the majority wins. Do these new instructions help you?"

"It sounds good to me. What about the questions?" I ask.

"Let me give you an answer soon." Tom laughs once more. Within weeks, I am assigned to the Executive Committee, which helps indicate the necessity of any policy changes and the perfect place to ask questions. Approximately two years later, Tom presents a new concept to the board, and it is accepted. The plan is to ensure direct coverage to underserved minority groups and women. The title is Strategic Partners Plan. The plan includes changes to the donor designations offering a more direct service to residents in the nine counties. There are three categories, one being the Community Impact Fund.

I resign as a board member and become the president of the African American Community Entrustment, or simply "The Entrustment." The focus is to work with our donors, the elder citizens, students, and to create partnerships to serve the community.

Our goal is to share the rich giving legacy of our ancestors, our donors, our families, and even strangers. When we say community, it has to mean an extension of families reaching out seeking the common good for everyone. We know, however, due to glaring statistics regarding the uneducated, disinherited, disconnected and economic disparity, some of our citizens struggle daily just to maintain a meager existence.

The Entrustment key major programs are forming partnerships to sponsor youth projects, Healthy Village Communities, Grandmothers Annual Event, Black History Month Students Essay Stories, and awarding twenty-four grants to non-profit agencies. Here are the following:

Five "Entrustment" Principles
1. People support what they help create.
2. Teamwork divides the task and doubles the success.
3. If you're too busy to help those around you succeed, you're too busy.
4. What affects everyone can best be solved by everyone.
5. African Americans can reach the moon by standing on each others shoulders!

Tom trains me to lead, offering the Ten Commandments of Leadership:
1. Always be up front.
2. Greet employees often.
3. Have responses ready.
4. Learn from the best people.
5. Keep your mouth shut with foolish people.

6. Never look fearful.
7. Relax completely.
8. Smile in every picture.
9. Walk around when thinking.
10. Quit when the fun stops.

P.S. Give 20 percent of your time and money helping others to be truly rich.

I follow President Ruppanner's guidance almost to the letter, especially the parts about relaxing and never looking fearful. Tom truly is the master of practicing common sense, lifting everybody up, and caring for all on an equal basis.

Curry Spice: The heart makes the inner man and woman now new, while shifting the emotions, the mind and the will too.

CHAPTER ELEVEN
2008–2009
A Dramatic Journey

January 19, 2008: Dr. Martin Luther King Jr. Essay and Poetry Contest

"This is the time of year that our thoughts and prayers turn to the commitment and sacrifices made by Dr. Martin Luther King Jr. We gather once again to celebrate the life and times of Dr. King. The North Central Neighborhood Association is celebrating the twenty-fourth year of our Dr. Martin Luther King Jr. Essay and Poetry Contest. Mrs. Lucy Cupp Pickens had the vision over twenty years ago to have this historical event. We wish to thank the contributors, donors, judges, parents, and teachers who jointly offer their unselfish support." Ethel Dailey-Burnside, president of the North Central Neighborhood Association, welcomes the participants of the contest.

Ethel and I became friends during the Super Saturday Community Event. Ethel is a community activist serving, senior citizens and young students for at least three decades. A major highlight of my life is serving as the master of ceremonies at the Annual Dr. Martin Luther King, Jr. Birthday Celebration.

At the celebration, the multicultural audience is in high gear. Approximately 239 students participate in the celebration. "Lift Every Voice and Sing," the black national anthem, opens every mind and heart as each person joins in praise for our fallen hero, Dr. MLK Jr. Rev. Lonnie Wallace prays for hope, peace, and unity among all human beings, and the recognition of special guests is valuable as the children prepare to read the winning speeches.

Dr. Emmett Carson, executive director of the Silicon Community Foundation, says, "Always strive for the best, and the best returns to you." Anita Webb is a community activist working with the North Central Neighborhood Association, as the official coordinator of the essay contest winners from grades one through nine. Anita loves to sing in the Pilgrim Baptist Church Choir whenever she and Arnold Webb, her husband, are not traveling. The students step proudly to the microphone and share their superb essays and poetry. The first-, second-, and third-place winners receive a savings bond, and the same winners in the high school student category receive cash awards.

"We Shall Overcome, " a famous song that is sung with the audience standing and holding hands, brings bittersweet memories of the years of the freedom marches in the 1960s and 1970s.

> "I have the audacity to believe that people everywhere can have three meals a day for their bodies, education and culture for their minds, and dignity, equality and freedom for their spirit." (Rev. Dr. Martin Luther King Jr., born 1929, died 1968)

In 2006 enters an interesting nonfiction memoir titled 'The Audacity of Hope' by Barack Obama. Is it only coincidental that both men have such audacity?

January 29: "An Evening to Remember ..."

The San Mateo Public Library presents "An Evening to Remember with Eleanor Curry, new author in San Mateo County." One of our guests, fascinated by the entire evening, grabs my hand and says, "You not only write, draw pictures, and tell oral history stories, you can even sing."

February 4: Eightieth Birthday Party, Red Carpet Style

Imagine my joy at having a hundred wonderful friends at my eightieth birthday party. It was held in early February 2008 at the San Carlos Adult Community Center.

My grown children and grandchildren host the birthday party for me and decide that it will be "a red carpet event." They took care of the entire evening, which included a hundred close friends who came by car or flew in from out of town and dressed to the nines. None came late. The conversations covered everything in sight:

- "Have Eleanor and Earl really been married sixty-two years?" Not till March; that's next month.
- "That looks like James Brown, the King of Soul!" It's Bruno Fleming, master of music, and Eleanor's son-in-law.
- "All the chocolate-and-caramel-skin teen waitresses have on white tops and black skirts." Those are the Curry's grandkids.
- "This food is delicious. The smothered chicken wings melt in your mouth. Who is the chef?" Marla, our granddaughter who came in from Laney College in Oakland, is the evening's chef.

- "I like to hear the rhythm of the drums. Do you know him?' Richmond is our first-born son.
- "Is that guy in white from head to toe, including his white patent leather shoes, a movie star?" That is John-John, one of our grandkids.
- "I hear somebody is going to roast Eleanor. Do you think it is her husband?" My oldest daughter, Brenda Davis, the comedienne, is the MC.
- "Do you live around here? How do you know the family?" Nancy Barker lives in Kelseyville, California, and we met at the school district in 1969. We last saw each other over thirty years ago.
- "Erma, who is that new man coming in the front door?" I ask. Erma replies, "It's your son Arnold flying in from Connecticut to surprise you."
- "My mother always knew lot about love but nothing about sex. How did they ever have all us kids? They didn't have time to tell us." Brenda, my first daughter, begins the evening program.
- "Where did Eleanor get that money hat?" Former mayor Claire Mack, of San Mateo, created the happy birthday hat.
- "Eleanor and I are both involved as community activists." Mayor Carole Groom from San Mateo brings greetings.
- "Seeing this wonderful multitude of family and friends, I see what Eleanor has been up to all these years. Yes, I love her." Richmond Earl, too filled with emotion, almost cries.
- "I have a special message I'd like to read to you from Oprah's friends wishing Mom the best birthday." Paul, another son, shares something wonderful.

- "Look there's Rev. Larry Ellis and First Lady Van from Pilgrim Baptist Church." Eleanor am one of the church's senior members.
- "Who is that white couple on the floor swing dancing?" They're Brice Hulling and Liz. Eleanor likes to collect people.
- "Someone is coming with a large gift and handing it to the Master of Music." Bruno opens the large box straight from Washington DC. Inside is a plaque that reads,

THE FLAG
OF THE
UNITED STATES
OF
AMERICA

This is to certify that the accompanying flag was flown
Over the United States Capitol at the request of the
Honorable Anna
G. Eshoo, Member of Congress.
This flag was flown in honor of Ms. Eleanor
Williams-Curry, on the joyous occasion of her 80th
Birthday.

February 2, 2008	Anna G. Eshoo
Date	Member of Congress

February 7: My Second-Oldest Daughter Has Cancer

The phone rings a week after the birthday party. Bonnie, our second-oldest daughter says, "Hi, Mom. I have some bad news for you." She is breathing rather deeply. "I had a pain in my lower back. The doctor told me I have cancer."

"What type?" I ask. I'm very concerned, but I don't want to frighten her.

"Mom, we're looking at alternatives," she says. "Don't be worried. I thought you should be the first to know. I'll tell the rest of the family and keep you posted."

I'm dumbfounded. I think of all the women I know who are cancer-survivors. I also realize that I neglected to get an answer regarding what type of cancer Bonnie has. Later, I find out that she has a rare type of cancer. Leiomyoma is a benign tumor composed of non-restricted, muscular tissue. It grows in the soft tissue of the body. It does not respond to chemotherapy or radiation, only surgery.

After six weeks of seeking alternatives methods, Bonnie decides to have surgery on May 5, 2008, at Kaiser Hospital in Sacramento, California. Two days after her surgery, I make my second trip to the hospital to relieve Charles, my son-in-law. Kaiser arranges for me to remain twenty-four/seven so I can assist and be with my daughter. I spent the night directly in her room. Together we pray, walk early in the morning when sleep is impossible, and rekindle our love. This is a most difficult struggle, yet my daughter remains brave throughout her ordeal.

June 2: San Mateo County
Democratic Central Committee

The SMCDCC headquarters is three blocks from my house in San Carlos and has seen forty years of community affairs, especially politics. Who would have believed that the primaries would run for twenty-one months? Hillary Rodham Clinton and Barack Obama are the top contenders for the Democratic nomination.

I am leaning toward Clinton. Earl, my husband, hollers from his lounge chair in front of the TV, "Eleanor! Come here quick. This new guy Obama is talking of the need for change."

"We have been waiting for things to change," Obama says, his voice firm and eager, yet steady. He pauses. "Ladies and gentlemen, we are the change we've been waiting for." The crowd bursts into deafening applause.

The next day, I arrive to volunteer at the SMCDCC, and Julie, a staff person, signs me in as a volunteer and discuss the items I decide to do, such as hours on duty, voter registration, and precinct walking. The same afternoon, I meet other volunteers. We become close friends even though I have a different schedule from most of them. Little did I know that I'd be taking a completely different course of action in my new task.

June 3: Who's 'I AM'?

"Do you honestly think Obama has a chance to become the presidential nominee for the Democratic Party, Mother dear?" Bruno, my son-in-law, seriously wonders.

"There's no doubt in my mind if 'I AM' wants him to win," I reply.

"Who's 'I AM'?" he asks. "I've never heard of this before." Bruno looks puzzled.

"Have you ever heard of Moses?" I ask.

"Yeah, he parted the Red Sea to save his people."

"Before that, Moses did not want to return to Egypt. I'll let my brother tell you the story."

After I reached Clifford, my eighty-four-year-old brother, a retired minister in Chicago, Illinois, with Bruno's question, Clifford quickly sent this message telling the background of 'I AM.'

"I AM is my name," declares God in the book
He wrote, revealing Himself as the Creator and

Sustainer of the Universe, in Genesis 1:1–7. When Moses said unto God, "The God of your fathers hath sent me unto you; and they shall ask me, what is his name? What shall I say unto them?"(Exodus 3:11) God said unto Moses, "I AM THAT I AM: and he said, Thus shalt thou say unto the children, "I AM hath sent me unto you" (Exodus 3:14).

Totally void of confusion, contradiction, or corruption, God speaks to his people. Disregarding magic, mystery, or myth, God speaks to his people. With grace, love, and peace, God speaks to his people. Laying aside all argumentation, confrontation, debate, presumption, and superstition, and remember God says, "I AM that I AM." Our inability or our rejection to "understand," God does nothing to lessen or eliminate the fact of His "I "AMNESS." God is without beginning or end, not bound by time but operating in it, having all power as in omnipotent: being present everywhere at the same time and with all infinite knowledge. Yes! I AM that I AM!

June 10: My Third-Oldest Daughter Has Cancer

The phone rings early in the morning from Gilroy. Barbara sounds upbeat, saying, "Hi, Mom. Bonnie is so much better since she had her surgery. I need to tell you something and ask for your help."

"Good morning," I say, still waking. "What's up?"

"I'm really doing well." Barbara starts talking faster. "The doctor told me I have cancer, too. I have to have a hysterectomy. The surgery is going to be June 25 at Stanford Hospital. Can you come and be with me?"

I'm wide awake now. "Of course. When did all this happen?"

"It happened a few years ago. I didn't think it was serious until my last visit. Will you be free, Mom? Are you too busy?"

"I'm never too busy for you guys," I say. "See you soon." I sit stunned at the news. "Lord, what am I going to do?" I begin to pray. I have signed up as a volunteer, but I will have to change my plans at the headquarters to be on call for both daughters.

While talking with the people at headquarters, April V., another staff member, says "Do you have any good ideas to promote Obama?"

"Yes," I say. "I can create a sixteen-inch square quilted pillow with the June third historical picture on it."

"Bring it so I can see it," she says. April is an interior designer.

The following Monday, the first pillow is ready. The design is solid red quilted cotton with the stars and stripes around the picture. The staff and several volunteers are excited about the idea. I decide to sell the pillows and donate a portion of the proceeds to the SMCDCC. I can complete approximately twelve pillows per week. The first person to get a pillow is a new friend, Mary T., who tells me later in a special note, "I still love having my red 'Obama pillow' made by you. I will treasure it as a handmade, one-of-a-kind present." I'm thrilled. I can stay home, make pillows, and still help take care of my daughters.

July 14: Commitment of Love

Today in the adult Sunday school class, Sister Joanne Griffith, the teacher, is discussing God's miracles. She turns to me, saying, "Sister Eleanor, are you aware of any present-day miracles?"

"Yes," I reply. "I have a close friend, Carl Brown, who is a quadriplegic. This means paralysis of all four limbs or of the entire body below the neck. His commitment to the Lord is amazing. When I first started going to visit with him, I thought I'd be able to lift his spirits, but he is so full of love for God that *he* inspires *me*. After I made a few Obama pillows, I decided to take him one as a gift. The minute he saw it, he ordered four more. Within weeks, he had ordered over fifteen. This young man never complains. He has to have twenty-four/seven health care. He finally sent one of the pillows to a girlfriend in Virginia. It seems that now that one of the pillows was going to be in the Washington, D.C. area. The miracle is God sending us a source straight to the City. There'll be some splendor at the bottom of the Capitol, too."

Sister Jeanne Brown asks, "How did you meet this young fellow?"

"I met Carl when he was six years old. He lived across the street from us. He played with our sons. When he turned seventeen, he asked my husband if he could get him a job.

"Once my husband took him to White Cliff Construction Company, he discovered that Carl could not read a ruler or a tape with numbers on it. However, Carl had a good attitude and was eager to learn. When the foreman threatened to fire Carl due to his lack of skills, my husband said emphatically, 'If you fire Carl, I go with him. Assign him to me; give me six months. I'll teach him to be a carpenter.' Two years later, Carl was a first-class carpenter. He became a manager, opened his own business, and worked on jobs all over the Bay Area. In 2003, he was hit in the back of the head while on his job, paralyzing his spine from the neck to his lower back. Carl is handsome with a smooth chocolate complexion. Prior to the accident, he was a body builder. Due to his taking extra good care of himself, he survived this severe crisis. If he had not been in top physical condition, Carl would not have survived. He remains in high spirits in spite of his condition."

Today, six years later, Carl's body remains ravaged by that accident, yet his spirit radiates immense joy. He smiles readily saying, "If this had not happened to me, I would not have found the real God and his son, Jesus Christ, who loves me."

LINKING RESOURCES AND PEOPLE

Barbara Conway, a young, Christian, African-American woman, considers herself to be blessed beyond the scope of the majority of African-American women. She lives in Foster City with her husband of thirty years, Allen Conway, and has one adult son, Marcus. She is articulate, self-assured, and authentic in her persona. She shares her personal thoughts regarding the new president, Barack Obama, after purchasing more than two dozen Obama pillows.

Barbara is inner directed as she confidently utters, "Two thousand eight is the year we never expected to see! When I saw the first Obama pillow, I was overjoyed with its beauty. Here was a creative way to share the excitement, happiness, and joy at a time in history of what we were witnessing from this highly intelligent young man. Who would have ever thought we'd live to see the day the United States would have an African American as president of the country. Can you believe you'd live to see this happen?" Barbara laughs, not waiting for the answer.

"I am one of the teachers of the adult women's class at Pilgrim Baptist Church in San Mateo. Before I retired in 2007, I was the director of employee services section at the Municipal Transportation Agency in San Francisco. Everybody calls it Muni for short. Now I'm a consultant in three areas: network marketing, health and wellness, plus the drug and alcohol field.

"I was attracted to the Obama pillows because of what we're going through right now. They convey a touchable human feeling. I immensely enjoy sharing these pillows. I gave several to some people I know and some I'd never seen, sometimes just to say thank you. My husband's ninety-four-year-old aunt called so happy, saying, 'Hello, hello, hello. Thank you, thank you, and thank you.'"

We Can't Find the Pillow Lady

The news of the pillows spreads. However, one item is missing: I didn't put any labels on the pillows. Monica Hollands, retail manager at the So Thankful clothing store in downtown San Mateo, tells me one sunny August afternoon, "Mama Curry, you won't believe what we found with Obama's and Michelle's picture on it. Not a T-shirt, but a beautiful red quilted pillow. Blanche Domino-Bailey, the stylish owner of Magic Fingers, was elated when she bought it. She was very disappointed because we only had one left. We don't know where she could get more.'"

"Oh, did you get it from Carl?" I ask. I'm thrilled to think she has found Carl.

"No, not Carl," she says. "It was on a couch at the Democratic headquarters in San Carlos. The big problem, though, is that we can't find the source that is making them."

"I'm the source." I'm smiling at Monica's discovery.

"You're the one? Are you telling the truth?" Monica hugs me too tightly, laughing. "We need some more pillows immediately!" she says. Within a week, Monica and Blanche order a dozen pillows, and Monica sells Obama accessories at the store. Suddenly her customers order the pillows in a variety of colors: red, white, and blue quilted materials and African designs. Monica and I become good friends, which is even more important. One day, while eating lunch, Monica flashes that uplifting smile of hers and says, "It's a good thing Obama ran for president or I might have missed getting to know you better, Mama Curry."

June 30: $700 Billion Bailout!

I'm getting calls from my family and many friends and am even getting stopped by some strangers in the shopping stores, all wondering what is happening with the financial world. What can the average citizen do, if anything?

Here's the message I sent to all those who struck up those conversations with me. I encouraged them to join my humble efforts.

"Let's pray that God heals our land," I write. "We ask God to stop the greed that is destroying our country. There will be no effective bailout without God's purpose, passion, and power. We are asking all God's people of faith to call on God for the next critical weeks!

"Please join us by talking to your family, coworkers, and friends. Start Tuesday, October 14, 2008, and continue through November 27, 2008, following the plan as listed below.

1. Pray every day for ten minutes to rid our homes first from any greed.
2. Fast every Wednesday from 7:00 a.m. to midnight, drinking liquids only.
3. Ask God to cleanse us, restore us, and use us.
4. Be generous and kind to someone you don't know.
5. Be prepared to celebrate God's grace and mercy this Thanksgiving Day. We cannot ignore God. We must not ignore God. We will not ignore

God in this enormous crisis. Thank you for joining our efforts."

We pass these fliers out at various gatherings. On October 12, 2008, when attending the church in Burlingame, California, Jill Goodman, one of my best spiritual friends for over forty years, invites me to pass the fliers out at her church. She explains to the congregation, "Eleanor brings us good news once again as we react in shock over the billion dollar bailout plan. She wants us to pray and fast. If you are so inclined, please do so."

Rev. Dr. James Noel was the speaker for the morning session, discussing "A Black Theological Reflection." He covered the African-American religious experience and the perspective of black theology on church and society, faith, and practice by focusing on three interrelated concepts that are central to the Reformed theological tradition and biblical criticism: covenant, kingdom, and empire.

"Today, before I get started on our session, I have been emotionally empowered already. An African American woman comes to a Euro-congregation to seek prayer for 'our country,'—not a black country, not a white country, but our country. The good news is that we need to pray for our country. The sociology of knowledge and what we look at are determined by our intimate view and/or our distraction. We all are receiving the same level of God and Jesus Christ. What is God saying to us about the others? In our presence today appears an African-American woman simply saying, 'We must pray and fast for our country.'"

Dr. Noel speaks to the need for all of us to think deeply while praying about "the others." Who are "the others"? Are the others in our midst, in other countries, right down the street, or some of our own relatives? Listening to Dr. Noel, my mind visualizes the phrase "one body, one soul, and one baptism."

Curry Spice: I speak to bring you joy. I tap dance to entertain.
            I sing to myself when I'm glad.
            I sing softly to ease the pain when I am sad.
            Most of all, I spread love with a smile,
            I use laughter and pleasant words to beguile.

CHAPTER TWELVE
2010–2011
Living Heaven on Earth

Heaven and Earth

Can we attempt to live on earth as it is in heaven? We all should have certain points in life when we know that if we follow God's plan for us, we shall have glimpses of living in heaven while on earth. We may not always fully understand what is going on; nevertheless, it is happening. One thing is for sure: I am the result of a long list of believers.

I ponder my stages of growth.

The year is 1942. Mother gives me her tattered Bible. "Keep this book close to you and try to live like you're told."

"What are you talking about?" I ask. "Where are you going?" I am teasing to ease the seriousness.

"We live and all of us shall die. This Bible will guide you through when I am dead and gone."

I took the book and tossed it in the corner near my bed. I have so much schoolwork that I lose track of it, seldom giving it a second thought.

It is now 1946. The mystery of God comes into our lives because Earl, my husband, is a praying man. God still feels vague to me.

"Eleanor, join me," Earl says. He kneels beside our bed. "We must pray and ask God to give us a healthy baby, with ten fingers and ten toes." Later, he comes to the hospital, counts ten fingers and ten toes, smiles, and says, "Thank God." He prays the same prayer over each of our children before they are born, and all of them are healthy. This seems like a miracle to me.

The year is 1955. Once again, Earl prays for a safe trip on his journey. We pack enough food to last him three days. A segregated law in different parts of the country makes traveling dangerous, so he seldom makes stops. He arrives three days later after driving nearly two thousand miles. He calls to tell me, "Thank God I made it." We are all safe in California before the year ends.

The year is 1956. God feels real to me due to my interacting with many people. How do we measure extra good neighbors? God places a multitude of situational people in our lives, yet we often underestimate their value to our growth. Think of the Henderson family, Pastor Richie, the believers in numerous churches, our teachers, and our close friends, all keeping us accountable to ourselves. I have tremendous faith in God.

What Is Faith?

"Faith is the substance of things hoped for, the evidence of things not seen.

Hebrews 11:1 King James Version

There are thirty-seven uses of this one word, *faith*, in the Bible. Yes, we have eyes to see, yet sometimes what we see is only a small portion of the total scene. We have ears, but who is listening? Faith is a fruit of the spirit, causing me to seek God's word daily and giving me strength when needed without a prior thought. Suddenly, God takes care of the situation.

What Is Hope?

Hope is another spiritual gift that puts our trust in God. I have hope in God. We can endure everything until the end of our earthly lives. We can live daily in healthy and healing ways. We can remain optimistic. We can seek peace for our families, friends, and neighbors. Or we can complain until we are no longer alive. We can eat and drink the wrong food, knowing it is not good for our bodies. Above all, we discover, if we view the world with fresh, open eyes every second, every minute, every day, the world looks full of hope. Our neighbors are right there in our sight, and we become rich in hope.

Who Is a Prayer Warrior?

A prayer warrior is a person who loves to spend time praying to God and talking to God. This is very personal, spending time in God's word. I read somewhere recently, 'God is not an emergency line' calling only when you need him. God is reachable twenty-four /seven, whether times or good or bad. He wants us close to him. Before I found God, my life was full of doubt and doing without. God turned me completely around, placing my feet on solid ground. What happens when you pray? The influence of prayer releases the blessings from God. When prayers go up; blessings come down. A prayer gets obedience from God, and steadfast takes this message to others. I pray for myself. I pray with others. I am a prayer warrior. I can shout "Hallelujah! Hallelujah! Hallelujah!"

Why Should You Pray?

Prayer releases God's awesome power. After working five to six days of a week, rest is required to have our energy replenished. Blessed assurance is a guarantee that all is well. Yesterday is over; get ready for tomorrow, which is today. Pray for courage to encourage others. Let us reason together, as we relieve the oppressed, guide our youth, and plead for the widow. These situations become our prayers.

What Is Love?

God's most magnificent gift of all is love. Love turns us from ourselves to others. The miraculous commitment to volunteering to help others is a contagious love. When I flash back to discover exactly when I first helped someone, I am only eight years old.

"Eleanor, we are going cross the walkway so you can meet our neighbor," Mother says. "She needs some help. I know you will be the perfect person." Mother looks for chances to be good to somebody.

"What can I do?" I ask.

"You know how to read." Mother smiles. "She can no longer see or even hold a book in her weak hands. Let's go now."

Mother takes me on my first trip to an eighty-two-year-old widow. I go once a week for nine weeks, and then she dies. Her mind remained strong as she told me stories. Who gained the most? I am stronger because of her stories, which the reading would trigger.

Another phase of life happenings centers on the workplace. Throughout the years, from being a waitress at fourteen years old and serving as a maid for ten dollars a day, I could not imagine the heights I would reach as better jobs kept appearing for me.

One of the toughest jobs that gives different rewards is being a wife and mother, without direct financial payback. Come on now. That is really positive love, unimaginable, unknown, and unseen. A young engaged woman, ask me, 'What can one do to keep a new husband happy'?

"Let him know he is more important than you are, and he will find out, you are more important than he is. Another thing, never be unhappy on payday." She laughs saying, "Makes no sense too me."

The year is 1983. I meet Rev. Larry Wayne Ellis. When our family living situation seemed as though it was coming unglued, I knew I had to get serious concerning God. We had just lost the house my husband had built in a foreclosure. We were devastated, not able to talk to each other. I began going to counseling, and I continued for a year. I thought. What else can go wrong? Too often, we do not come to God until something dreadful happens. I am guilty of such behavior. Before, I actually believed I could 'do all things,'. Then I turned to God, adding "through Christ which strengthens me." I surrender to God. Praise God for his grace and mercy.

My life turned around when I was thirty-two years old in 1960. We had our eight children baptized, but my feet were on shaky ground. Slowly I became a backslider, going to worship very little during the next fifteen years. I kept reading my Bible, not fully understanding its words yet feeling that it made sense.

The situation that caused me to suffer brought me to Pilgrim Baptist Church in 1986. What happened? My vague connection to God was gone. Before long, I was stumbling through life, hoping I was doing the right thing, believing what others thought of me.

Another test came to our family in 2009. Bonnie, our second daughter, found out the cancer had returned to her body. We began a nonstop, twenty-four/seven schedule, with her being the entire focus. Her husband, siblings, and grandchildren surround her daily.

In the meantime, another test came for me. My voice started fading away, and the doctors said it might be a minor stroke caught in time. I spent forty-eight hours in the emergency service unit at Kaiser Hospital in Redwood City, CA. Once released, I was told not to drive too far alone, or beyond a dozen miles from home, which caused a problem with my plans to be with my daughter. I could not make the two-hour drive to Elk Grove where Bonnie lives. I prayed for an answer. Two days later, Bonnie and I started talking on the telephone from midnight to early in the morning, twice a week. I picked up before three rings. She loved those times with just the two of us. Although she was in debilitating pain, she told me, "Mom, I want you to know, love from all of you is keeping me alive."

On February 2, Charles, Bonnie's husband, called at seven thirty in the morning, saying, "Bonnie is upset and talking irrationally. She's hollering for you."

"Let me talk to her," I said.

"She is not making sense …"

"I'll handle it," I interjected. "Put her on the phone."

"Mama, Mama, can you come get me?" she said. "I have to get out of here now. Please help me get away."

"We'll get you out before dinnertime today," I told her.

"I called Brenda already," Bonnie said. "She is on her way. Mama, what are you going to do?"

"Relax until Brenda gets there. We'll take care of you. I love you." I hung up the phone, and an instinct came over me. I bowed my head and clasped my hands, and standing still, I prayed, crying, asking God to take over for me. Get her out safely. Meanwhile, Barbara and her son Sterling were on their way. They stopped thirty minutes from Bonnie and also prayed for her. Brenda had reached Bonnie by this time and started calling Barbara for help. God was moving the scenes. Charles was undecided about whether to keep her home or let her leave. He decided to let her go to be with Barbara in Gilroy.

They arrived at Barbara's at five o'clock that evening. Bonnie called me the minute she was able.

"Hello, Mama!" she said. "How did you get me here before dinnertime, as you promised?"

"God moves suddenly," I answered. "He took care of it."

The next few days were critical for her. She called emergency services at one point to come get her at midnight, still in enormous pain. Once more, various family members went to her bedside, two at a time. We learned that the cancer was choking her, causing her trouble breathing. She decided on February 9 that she felt free from all burdens for the first time ever. "Yes. I am free," she said. She told Barbara not to fret over her anymore. She wanted nothing else to stop the pain because, for her, it was over. She knew that God was ready for her to come to heaven.

Barbara called at 4:30 a.m. on February 14, 2010, to tell me that Bonnie had gone to sleep. I cry while thanking God for letting her go home to heaven. We'll love her always.

I am humble. I have new meaning with the growth of a closer relationship with not only God but also his beloved son, Jesus Christ, my Lord and Savior, and the holy- spirit. The holy-spirit is the true way we are ever close to God. Believe me, this is eternal living. I am connected, I belong, and I encourage you to start living in God's magnificent universe with him. My life is proactive, not reactive. I pray daily on purpose. God has me under his wings. God sends us angels of love. I feel His total love. I never knew my place until God opened the door of my heart.

Curry Spice: Are you looking for your place? Try God!

The End

"Everybody can be great because anybody can serve.
You only need a heart full of grace and
a soul generated by love "
Rev. Martin Luther King Jr.
We thank God for an empowering new year.